PACKAGING
DESIGN

Chris van Uffelen

PACKAGING DESIGN

BRAUN

Preface

The wide range of hugely varied packaging projects displayed in this book introduces the reader to the world of packaging design. At first glance, packaging appears to serve a purely functional purpose. However, packaging can also be viewed as the 'face' of a product and is the first thing to be seen by potential consumers. A product's packaging must fulfill a number of primary functions, including providing a transportable container that can be easily stored and stacked, as well as protecting the contents against dirt or mechanical and climate-related factors. The degree of protection needed depends on the specific product. Furthermore, secondary functions must also be catered for; any packaging must provide information such as amounts and weights, as well as a bar code or EAN code. In the case of food packaging, the ingredients and sell-by-date must also be displayed. Sometimes packaging is also designed not only to protect the product, but also to protect the consumer, for example from sharp edges or hazardous substances.

Packaging must be simple to fit and easy to remove and in some cases should not be resealable. Some products, liquids for example, are divided into saleable amounts in containers such as tubes or bottles. The packaging determines the Unit Load, making logistic processes and trade easier. A further functional use is conservation of the product, for example by using vacuum packaging or packaging a product in sterile containers. Additionally, the packaging also helps to protect the product from manipulation or theft. Last but not least, packaging also makes the product easier to use, for example with cleaning fluids, where the correct amount can be measured out directly.

Another central theme in this book is the role that packing plays in promoting a product. Packaging must catch the consumer's eye; its sculptural appearance, color, additional images or graphics must set the product apart from the competition. As a result, the search for a package that suits the product's image is a fundamental part of marketing any new product. The packaging must serve the quick and easy identification of the product and give the brand an effective profile. The product's name must be eye-catching and the logo placed in a prominent position, or the package itself must characterize the product.

Eye-catching, representative packaging can significantly increase the popularity of a product. In terms of a product's marketability, this is of greater importance than the package's functionality. As a result, a second packaging shell is often wrapped around the actual functional packaging. Although this is not particularly environmentally friendly, it is understandable. Consequentially, many examples of packaging included in this volume concern themselves with ecological aspects of a practice that is in itself not environmentally friendly. Particular importance is given to high-end and sometimes pricey luxury jewelry packaging, where it is important to emphasize the value of the packaged product. A perfume bottle gives the product its identity - whether romantic, elegant or sporty. Limited editions, where only the packaging, and not the product itself, is different, can also fuel purchase incentive.

Food

Food containers are of particular importance when it comes to package design as these must cater to a number of rules and regulations. The goods contained are often perishable so packaging has to offer maximum protection. It is not only the manufacturing but also the filling process that are subject to strict regulations. Furthermore, compulsory food labels must provide the consumer with information about the contents and the composition of the product, in order to protect both the health and interests of the buyer. New packaging materials (intelligent packaging) are capable of changing color, indicating the deterioration or spoilage of a product.

Other features of food packaging include numerous examples of voluntary information about the manufacturer, pertaining to the specific characteristics of the product, such as its origins or the manufacturing process; this is intended to give a competitive advantage. Instructions for use are also often included. Product-specific packaging sizes also deserve a mention, as these, though not compulsory, are often expected by the consumer. It is also worth noting that packages intended for sale in a supermarket should be easy to stack and store.

When it comes to food packaging, one of the most demanding products has to be the raw egg. This requires maximum mechanical protection and the package has to compensate for the unwieldy nature of the goods and its natural characteristics. It is the desire to overcome these difficulties that has resulted in the frequent appearance of egg packaging in this chapter. The banana, unlike the egg, is not represented at all in this volume. The packaging in this case grows with the product, can be opened easily, and is clearly recognizable thanks to its distinctive color and shape.

Another special feature specific to food packaging is that customers are not permitted to open the packaging and there are often no open examples for customers to sample. As a result, many food packages include a picture of the goods inside or incorporate a window. However, numerous high-end products do not include this window, choosing instead to leave the product hidden, thus giving it a certain mysteriousness. Some packages use a window to incorporate the product itself into the graphic design. Particularly interesting in this chapter is the inclusion of various environmentally friendly packages made from folded paper or card. These are made without glue and are often inspired by nature.

Ceylora Cinnamon

This simple design is a packaging solution for dried cinnamon sticks. Made from card, the box has been transformed into the shape of an apple, all without using any kind of glue. The package is sealed with a small piece of real cinnamon. The natural colors and tones reinforce the association of the package shape with an apple and emphasize the natural rather than manufactured quality of the product contained within.

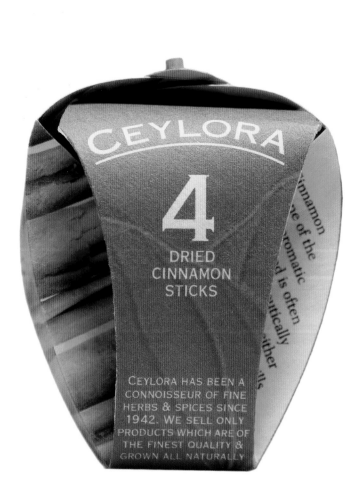

DESIGNER: Dominic Flask (USA)
YEAR OF DEVELOPMENT: 2008
MAIN MATERIAL: paper

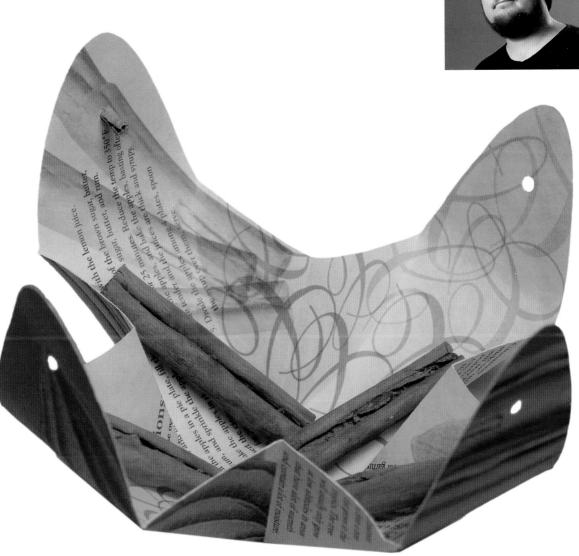

**Design:
Dominic Flask**

DESIGNER: Neosbrand (Spain)
DISTRIBUTOR: Blanc Gastronomy
YEAR OF DEVELOPMENT: 2010
MAIN MATERIAL: glass

Blanc Oro

Oro is a premium oil made by Blanc.
This innovative and unmistakable product
with four-karat gold chips is unique
on the market. Its design packaging is
characterized by a minimalistic style
and Swarovski crystals, which strengthen
its exclusivity.

Design: Neosbrand

Chocolate Packaging for New Year Gift

The task was to create New Year holiday wrapping paper for this corporate gift candy bar. Whilst working on the packaging, the designer was inspired by the Chinese calendar and Japanese origami. According to the Chinese calendar 2011 was the year of the rabbit so the designer decided to create a wrapping paper, which can be transformed into an origami rabbit after use. The designer also wanted to highlight a careful attitude towards paper and emphasize that it can be recycled. The inscription on the wrapper says: "Don't throw the wrapper away. You can make a origami bunny out of it." A instruction leaflet is attached under the wrapper.

Design: Ramin Hasanalizade

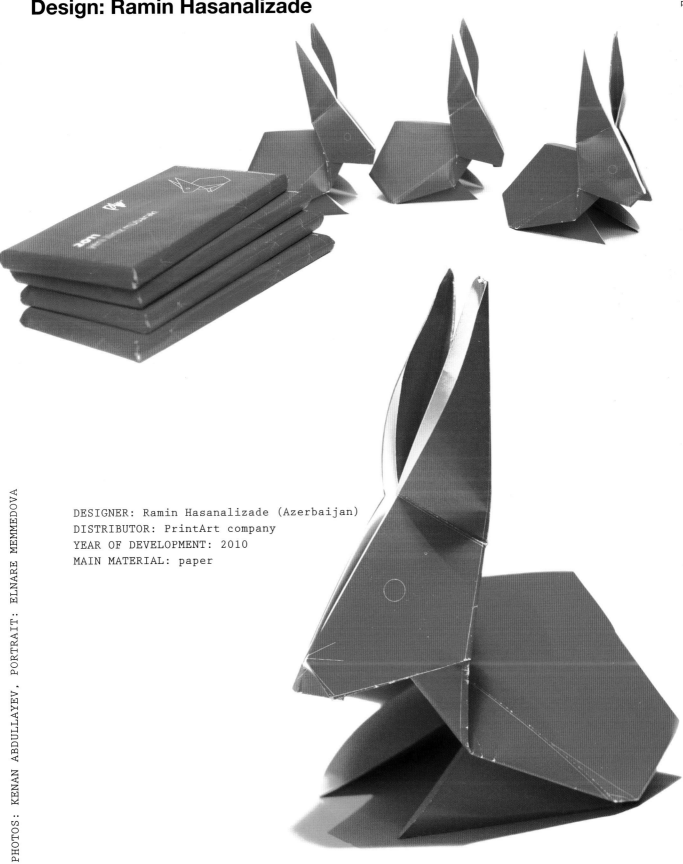

DESIGNER: Ramin Hasanalizade (Azerbaijan)
DISTRIBUTOR: PrintArt company
YEAR OF DEVELOPMENT: 2010
MAIN MATERIAL: paper

PHOTOS: KENAN ABDULLAYEV, PORTRAIT: ELNARE MEMMEDOVA

Maggi

Design: Julius Maggi

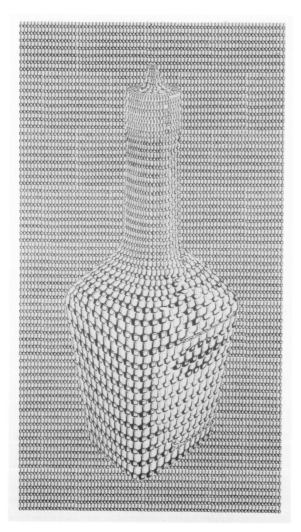

Visionary business man Julius Maggi not only developed the recipe for this piquant sauce but also its iconic bottle design: the four-cornered brown glass bottle with its red top and yellow sticker and the four-pointed star. The product itself has barely changed since the beginning of the industrial era in the 19th century until today. Only the yellow sticker has undergone some minimal changes. In the 1990s the Maggi seasoning became a design object. In 1995 Maggi organized the "First European Design Competition for Kitchen and Tableware". Over 300 design schools and freelance designers were invited to get creative with the Maggi seasoning.

DESIGNER: Julius Maggi (Switzerland)
DISTRIBUTOR: Maggi GmbH
YEAR OF DEVELOPMENT: 1886
MAIN MATERIAL: glass, paper

| 1886 | 1907 | 1914 | 1917 | 1919 | 1924 | 1928 | 1937 | 1943 |

1946   1947   1957   1959   1965   1977   1980   1987   2011

Wishes Project

The idea behind this design was the development of a new means of communication between the designers and other creative companies. Instead of sending a mail to prospective collaborators, the designers have developed a gold-colored box, divided into nine separate sections. Each box contains a slice of cake and a small gold coin with the famous Cannes' Lion on it. The designers wanted to offer "only the best" to creative directors so each box contains a short greeting message: "We wish you only the best of 2012".

DESIGNER: Nick and Jack (France)
DISTRIBUTOR: Nick and Jack
YEAR OF DEVELOPMENT: 2012
MAIN MATERIAL: gold paper 225 g/m³

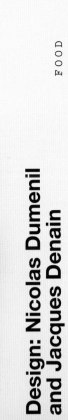

**Design: Nicolas Dumenil
and Jacques Denain**

5 Olive Oil

Design: Designers United

There was no specific brief from the management team regarding the target market or price, the designers just knew that they needed to come up with a good design proposition for a new series of high-quality extra virgin olive oil intended for the international market to be positioned as a premium olive oil but at a reasonable price. The designers came up with a solution that is elegant and contemporary but at the same time reminiscent of old potion bottles. While looking for an appropriate brand name the designers came up with the number 5, symbolizing olive oil as the 'fifth element'.

DESIGNER: Designers United / Dimitris Koliadimas, Dimitris Papazoglou (Greece)
DISTRIBUTOR: World Excellent Products S.A.
YEAR OF DEVELOPMENT: 2011
MAIN MATERIAL: glass, cork

FIVE
Ultra premium
extra virgin
olive oil

FIVE
Organic
extra virgin
olive oil

Superior category Greek Gourmet o
from hand picked, sustainably grow
by mechanical means. 5 organic is
maintaining its excellent and intac
valuable components of natural o

Bottled for **WORLD EXCELLENT PR**
2 Kepelian Agra St., 570 09 Kalochi
www.wep-sa.com

Product of Greece

Store in a cool, dry place,
away from direct sunlight
Best before: see imprint

FIVE
Organic
extra virgin
olive oil

FIVE
Organic
extra virgin
olive oil

premium
virgin
oil

RENDERINGS: COURTESY OF THE DESIGNERS, PORTRAIT: CHRYSA NIKOLERI, THESSALONIKI

La Nevateria

Design: Bisgràfic

La Nevateria is a shop that sells confectionary and coffee. This striking packaging design divideds the boxes into two colors; brown symbolizes the coffee itself, while the various bright colors reference the sweets inside. The boxes look great on their own or when arranged as a group and their simple but bright appearance is designed to catch the customers' eye.

DESIGNER: Bisgràfic (Spain)
CLIENT: La Nevateria
YEAR OF DEVELOPMENT: 2011
MAIN MATERIAL: cardboard

Ikea Food Skarpsill

Ikea is a worldwide Swedish home furnishing company with 267 stores attracting a total of 590 million visitors annually. Ikea's private food label was introduced in 2006, focusing on Swedish recipes made with quality products to a low price. The products are sold at Ikea stores all over the world. The product range is aimed at attracting food lovers who are interested and curious about different food cultures, particularly Swedish ones. The packaging should provoke interest in the product as well as present it in a clear, honest and appetizing way. The product should express the key values: reliability, quality, Swedishness.

DESIGNER: Stockholm Design Lab (Sweden)
DISTRIBUTOR: Ikea Food
YEAR OF DEVELOPMENT: 2011
MAIN MATERIAL: tin

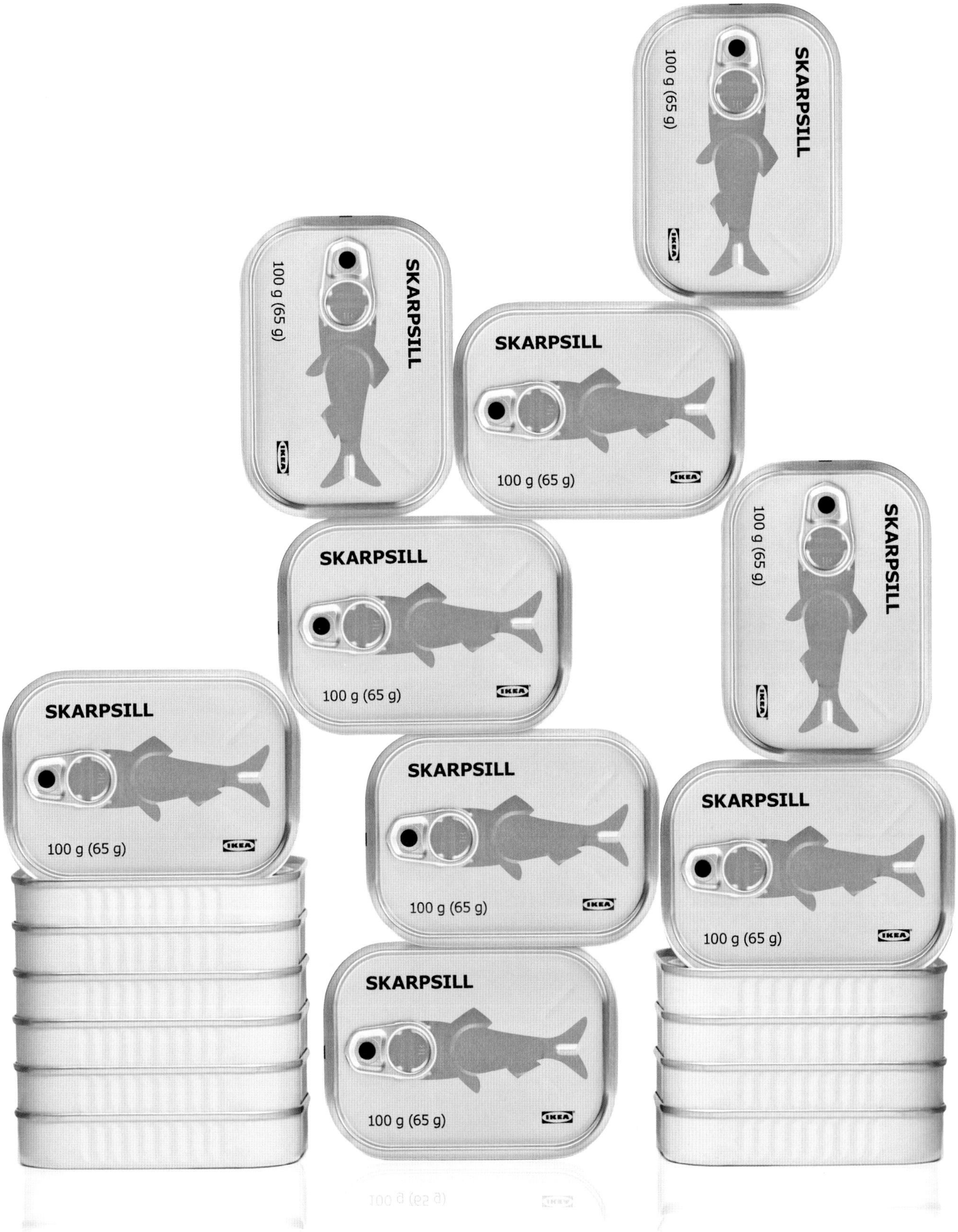

PHOTOS: COURTESY OF THE DESIGNERS

Generative Salt

During research on salt, the designer discovered that salt actually plays a much bigger and important role in our lives than we realize; salt can be found in almost any chemical element around us in varying amounts. The designer decided to focus on four chemical elements and visualize the changing of the salt in each one of them. The data was the fed into a generative software system, producing five different packages. The first is the base of the other four, all of which represent a different chemical element: Potassium, aluminum, bromine and magnesium. Additionally, each package is decorated with an abstract drawing of the chemical element it represents. This project was part of a third-year packaging course in the visual communication department at Shenkar, Israel; under the guidance of Tamar Mani.

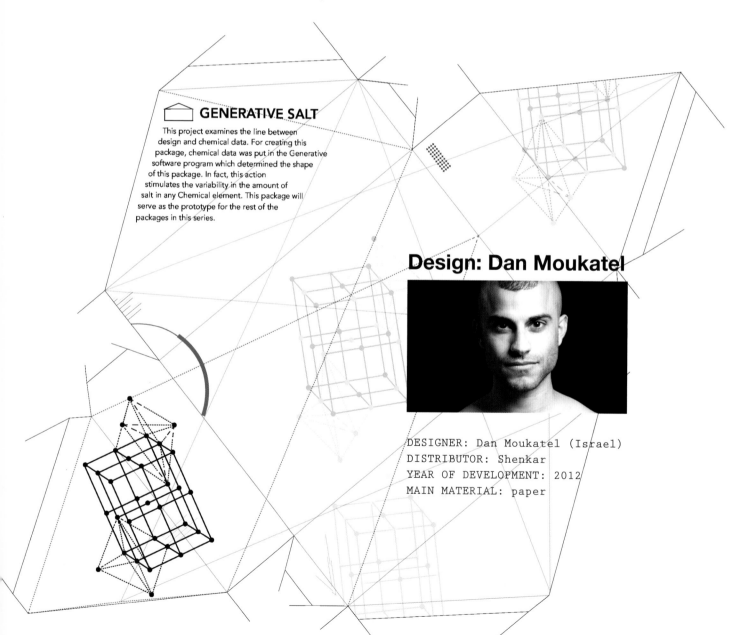

GENERATIVE SALT

This project examines the line between design and chemical data. For creating this package, chemical data was put in the Generative software program which determined the shape of this package. In fact, this action stimulates the variability in the amount of salt in any Chemical element. This package will serve as the prototype for the rest of the packages in this series.

Design: Dan Moukatel

DESIGNER: Dan Moukatel (Israel)
DISTRIBUTOR: Shenkar
YEAR OF DEVELOPMENT: 2012
MAIN MATERIAL: paper

Mambajamba

Mambajamba is a new take on the traditional animal cracker. The exterior design features a cropped illustration of animals' eyes that is revealed as a pop up when the box flips open. Each box pairs two flavors together in two separate compartments that become accessible once the box has been opened.

DESIGNER: Meg Eaton (USA)
DISTRIBUTOR: prototype
YEAR OF DEVELOPMENT: 2009
MAIN MATERIAL: paper board

Design: Meg Eaton

What animal am I?!
I live in swamps
Frogs & turtles are tasty snacks
I am cold blooded
My back feet are webbed
I have about 80 teeth

Chocolate Box

Design: Haylee Powers

The inspiration for this design came from the beauty of the chocolates that were to be contained within it. The designer wanted to design a box that would tempt the consumer to purchase the chocolates. The bright orange color contrasts the white box, while the folded top gives the design an elegant, inviting appearance.

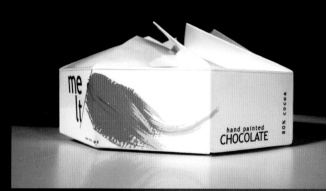

DESIGNER: Haylee Powers (USA)
DISTRIBUTOR: prototype
YEAR OF DEVELOPMENT: 2009
MAIN MATERIAL: laminated paper

Gogol Mogol

Boiling eggs can be very time consuming, so Gogol Mogol is a new way of cooking, storing and packing eggs. The package design enables storeowners to sell eggs by arranging them in a vertical position. Each individual package for an egg is made with several layers. Under the first layer is the catalyst that produces heat when activated. When the consumer pulls out the membrane by stretching a tag, a chemical reaction between takes place and the egg begins to heat up. So, in a few minutes, when you open the cover of the egg package, you have a boiled egg.

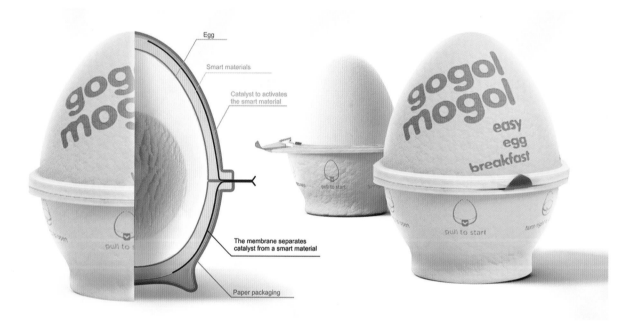

DESIGNER: Kian branding agency (Russia)
DISTRIBUTOR: prototype
YEAR OF DEVELOPMENT: 2011
MAIN MATERIAL: recycled cardboard

Design:
Kian branding agency

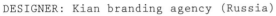

Quick Fruit

The idea behind the Quick Fruit
packaging is that of a fruit sliced in
half showing the core of it as the lid
of the product. A clean, simple logo
with the letter "Q" depicting a cup with
a spoon appears on the lid and side.
This concept was visualized and rendered
in a three-dimensional package with
added photographic elements such as the
kiwi fruit.

DESIGNER: Marcel Buerkle /
Circum Punkt Design (South Africa)
YEAR OF DEVELOPMENT: 2008

Design: Marcel Buerkle

Quick® Kiwi
Real fruit in flavoured jelly

A delicious, healthy and convenient ready-to-eat serving of real fruit in flavoured jelly • Contains no preservatives, no artificial colours and flavours, no artificial sweeteners and no added cane sugar • Best served chilled •

LIFT TO OPEN

Quick® Kiwi
fruit in flavoured je

Sustainable Origami Food Box

Design: Michealle Renee Lee

This packaging is for a mobile eatery that serves rice meals. The idea was to bring delight through the act of discovery when opening the package. The distinctive form is easily recognizable. When closed, the form resembles a bud. As it opens, the folds slide into a full-bloomed flower to reveal the colorful contents. It has a self-closing mechanism that glides into close and open position with minimal effort for ease of manipulation. For comfort and stability, the shape and size of the box fits perfectly into the palm of the hands, while the octagonal sides make for better grip. For convenience, the box can be laid flat, like a plate, to prevent food from getting caught in the corners.

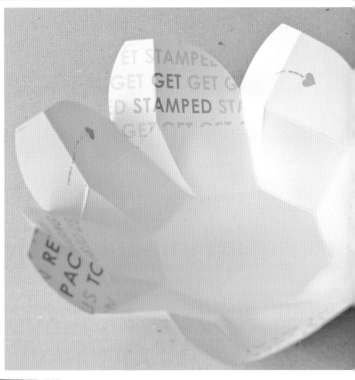

DESIGNER: Michealle Renee Lee (Philippines)
DISTRIBUTOR: Primatech Paper Solutions
YEAR OF DEVELOPMENT: 2011
MAIN MATERIAL: paperboard

Ritter Sport

Ritter Sport is a family-run company, founded by Eugen Ritter and Clara Göttle in 1912. In 1932 Clara Ritter invented Ritter Sport's trademark feature: a square-shaped chocolate bar that could fit into a pocket and wouldn't break as easily as the traditional long chocolate bar. The Ritter Sport brand was further developed by the introduction of a color palette and Alfred Otto Ritter allocated each flavor to its own individual color. The revolutionary snap-pack packaging set Ritter Sport apart from the competition. The company went on to be the first to replace aluminum and paper packaging with recyclable polypropylene. Nowadays, the company is renowned for the high quality of its products, advertised under the slogan "Quality. Chocolate. Squared."

DESIGNER: Clara Ritter (Germany)
DISTRIBUTOR: Ritter Sport
YEAR OF DEVELOPMENT: 1932
MAIN MATERIAL: polypropylene foil for snap-pack

1932

1960

1969

1974

1978

1981

Design: Clara Ritter

Erdbeer Joghurt

Halbbitter

Rum Trauben Nuss

Marzipan

Voll-Nuss

Knusperflakes

Weisse Voll-Nuss

Joghurt

Ganze Mandel

Pfefferminz

Alpenmilch

Edel-Vollmilch

Nugat

1987

2000

2007

Premium Packaging for Premium Products

Coop Switzerland has for many years pursued a clearly structured own-label strategy through which the company has complemented the branded products in its range. One of these lines is positioned in the upper segment, both with regard to quality and price, and includes foods as well as kitchen utensils and creative tableware. Featuring a unique design, these products are marketed under the "Fine Food" brand label in all of the Coop stores. The design is essentially characterized by a silvery surface for text and technical information, a black strip containing the brand name and a range of images defined specifically for these products. All of the food products come with a small information leaflet in which the history of the respective product is explained.

DESIGNER: Jean Jacques Schaffner (Switzerland)
YEAR OF DEVELOPMENT: 2005
MAIN MATERIAL: paperboard
CLIENT: Coop Genossenschaft

FINE FOOD | DESIGN

DINNER FOR 6

24-TEILIGE BESTECKGARNITUR FÜR 6 PERSONEN
MÉNAGÈRE 24 PIÈCES POUR 6 PERSONNES
SERVIZIO DI POSATE DA 24 PEZZI PER 6 PERSONE

FINE FOOD | DESIGN

IL DOLCE

6 KUCHENGABELN
6 FOURCHETTES À DESSERT
6 FORCHETTE DA DOLCE

Design:
Jean Jacques
Schaffner

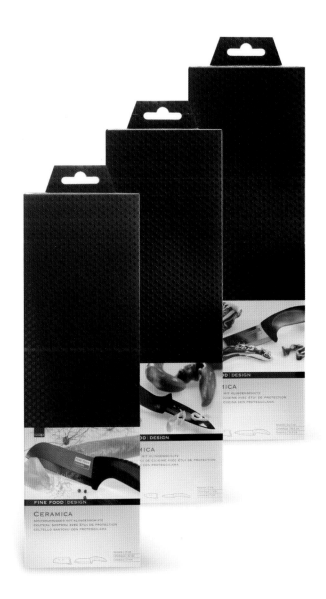

FINE FOOD | DESIGN

CERAMICA

Butter! Better!

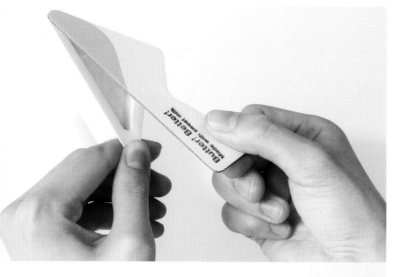

Butter! Better! is an innovative take on portable butter. It comprises triangular-shaped packages made of plastic with a wooden knife that is adapted to fit the shape of the packet and serves as a lid. The built-in knife eliminates the hassle of bringing your own cutlery. The package is easy to open and use.

DESIGNER: Yeongkeun Jeong (South Korea)
DISTRIBUTOR: prototype
YEAR OF DEVELOPMENT: 2010
MAIN MATERIAL: wood, plastic

Design: Yeongkeun Jeong

Butter! Better!
Made with sweet milk

Hive Eggs

Design: Chaiyasit Tangprakit

This egg box can be assembled without the use of adhesives and is fully recyclable. The handle makes the box easier to carry than the more traditional egg box design currently widely used. The interior compartments are interlinked, giving them additional strength and stability and stopping the eggs from moving and becoming damaged during transportation. The design is simple and easy to use but has a fresh new appearance, a great improvement on traditional egg packaging, which comes open more easily and is not as stable.

DESIGNER: Chaiyasit Tangprakit (Thailand)
DISTRIBUTOR: prototype
YEAR OF DEVELOPMENT: 2012
MAIN MATERIAL: kraft paper

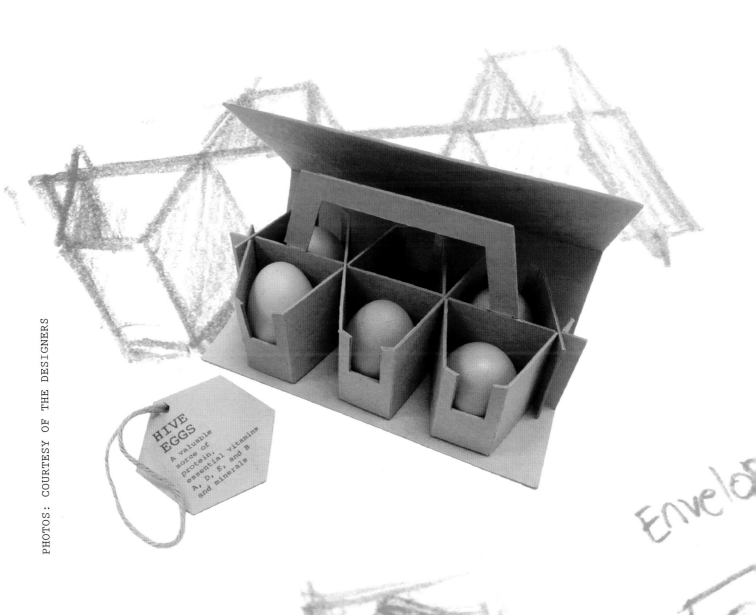

Envelo

Mighty Nuts

Design: Maija Rozenfelde

This package for pistachios tells a narrative in every detail. The shape and opening mechanism is an abstract reference to pistachios themselves. An important part is the focus on user experience and secondary function of the package. The result is a package with an inside tray that holds pistachios and an outer part that becomes a tray for the shells - a perfect way to enjoy pistachios instantly. The graphics are no less important. The intention behind the hand-made product was to create graphics that depict the crunchiness of pistachios. The engraved design is aesthetically appealing and functional, as the nutrition facts are shown on the front panel.

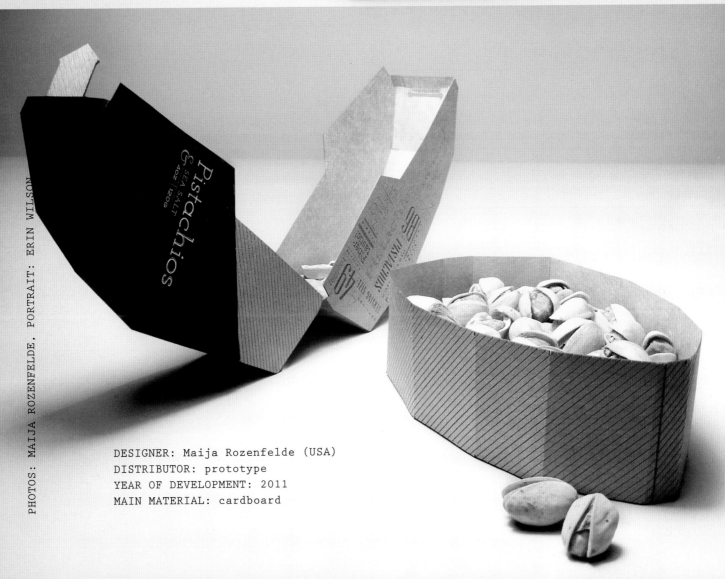

PHOTOS: MAIJA ROZENFELDE, PORTRAIT: ERIN WILSON

DESIGNER: Maija Rozenfelde (USA)
DISTRIBUTOR: prototype
YEAR OF DEVELOPMENT: 2011
MAIN MATERIAL: cardboard

Evolve Organic Oil

SabotagePKG designed the brand and identity for this new range of premium, organic, cold pressed oils by Evolve. The brief was to create an ecological-premium brand identity, which embodies this ethos.

Sabotage developed a chic carafe style glass bottle complete with integral lid and pour spout. The bottle has been designed with reuse in mind and in this way reducing ecological impact, oil refills come in a sealed fresh pouch. The base oil range includes Hemp Seed, Walnut, Apricot Kernel & Pumpkin Seed each individually identifiable by a color code system.

DESIGNER: SabotagePKG (United Kingdom)
DISTRIBUTOR: Evolve
YEAR OF DEVELOPMENT: 2011
MAIN MATERIAL: glass, plastics, laminated pouch

ORGANIC
COLD PRESSED OIL
HEMP SEED

330 ml 11.16 fl.oz

ORGANIC
COLD PRESSED OIL
WALNUT

330 ml 11.16 fl.oz

Design: SabotagePKG

PHOTOS: STUDIO 21 PHOTOGRAPHY, LONDON, PORTRAIT: BEN FISHER, LONDON

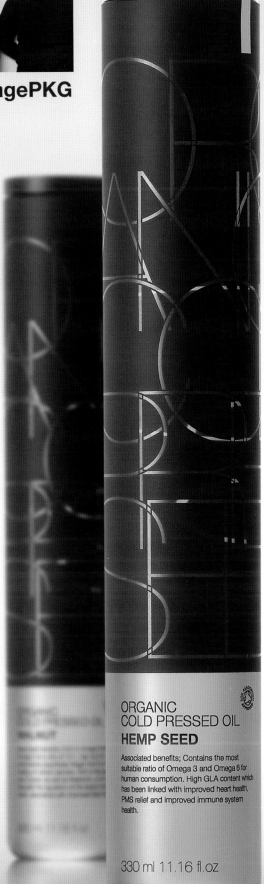

ORGANIC
COLD PRESSED OIL
HEMP SEED

Associated benefits; Contains the most
suitable ratio of Omega 3 and Omega 6 for
human consumption. High GLA content which
has been linked with improved heart health,
PMS relief and improved immune system
health.

330 ml 11.16 fl.oz

ORGANIC
COLD PRESSED OIL
APRICOT KERNEL

Associated benefits; High Iron, Fibre and
Omega 9 content. High in essential fatty acids,
Linoleic Acid, Oleic Acid and the very potent
Vitamin E that is known to boost skin health.
High content of Vitamin B17, Laetrile, that has
been linked with cancer prevention.

330 ml 11.16 fl.oz

MousseTube

DESIGNER: Saana Hellsten (Finland)
CLIENT: The Institute of Packaging
Starpack Awards 2008
DISTRIBUTOR: prototype
YEAR OF DEVELOPMENT: 2008
MAIN MATERIAL: carton for liquids

MousseTube is a packaging for children's food - mousse, yoghurt etc. - made of carton for liquids. It won silver in The Institute of Packaging Starpack Awards 2008. Saana Hellsten wanted to create a solution for the problem that many yoghurt cups, for example, are often too big for little children to eat at once. MousseTube is easy to carry with you and have as a snack wherever without having to eat it all at once and without needing a spoon as the child can squeeze the food straight into their mouth. The white color decorated with cute animal characters gives the packaging a fresh look and makes it appealing to children. There are no sharp corners and the product is completely recyclable.

**Design:
Saana Hellsten**

Peach mousse
Calcium - Vitamin D - Protein
eat well

Blueberry mousse
Calcium - Vitamin D - Protein
eat well

Banana mousse
Calcium - Vitamin D - Protein
eat well

Migros Sélection

Schneiter meier developed the Migros Sélection premium line for a leading Swiss supermarket chain, providing everything from naming, to design concept, to realization of each individual package. The common design features - emotive imagery, classic gold frieze, visual humor and empty space - give the product line a strong character and distinctive look that stands out on the shelves. The Migros Sélection product line has grown significantly over the past two years and now includes around 300 items in the food section.

DESIGNER: schneiter meier / Andy Schneiter, Cornelia Mayer, Andrea Jenzer, Christian Guler (Switzerland)
DISTRIBUTOR: Migros-Genossenschafts-Bund
YEAR OF DEVELOPMENT: 2005-2012
MAIN MATERIAL: paper

MIGROS Sélection
Carnaroli Risotto

MIGROS Sélection
Riz Basmati

MIGROS Sélection
Riz Camargue rouge

MIGROS Sélection | Salame al tartufo | Salami aux truffes
Salami mit Trüffeln
Salame al tartufo

MIGROS Sélection | Viande séchée de cerf | Viande séchée de cerf
Hirschtrockenfleisch
Carne secca di cervo

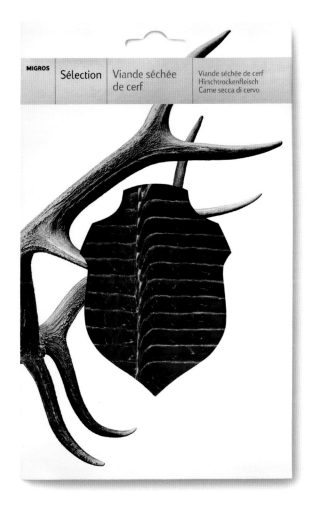

Trata on Ice

The tail of the fish is one of the main visual elements used on this frozen seafood packaging series. It was used both for the design of the logo and the structure of the packages. It is a very strong element of the brand since it makes the products recognizable from any view angle. The black background, the subtle typography and the seafood illustrations were used in order to emphasize the quality of the product and to give a delicatessen feeling. Consumers can actually see the product through the holes on the illustrations that highlight the type of seafood that is inside the package.

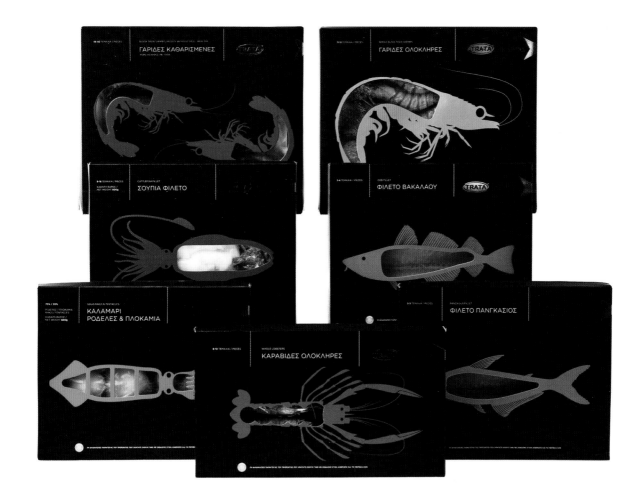

Design: Beetroot

DESIGNER: Beetroot (Greece)
DISTRIBUTOR: KONVA
YEAR OF DEVELOPMENT: 2010
MAIN MATERIAL: paper

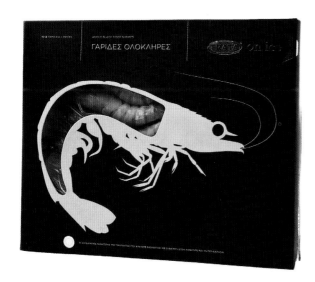

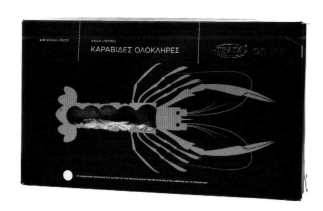

Helios

Helios has been the leading brand for ecological, biodynamic and environmentally friendly products on the Norwegian market since 1969. The products were mainly sold through specialty stores for ecological food. In 2010 it was decided that Helios would be sold in grocery stores. This set the stage for a repositioning of the brand, enabling it to compete better with fast moving consumer goods found in bigger stores. Uniform designed a prominent new logo that emphasizes the meaning of the word Helios (sun God). The logo was designed to be recognized quickly across different product groups and in a chaotic store environment. The new illustrations and fresh colors build a strong brand that consumers love. Developed under consultant Erik Jansson and project manager Pia Falk Lind.

DESIGNER AND ILLUSTRATOR: Cecilie Berg Børge-Ask (Norway)
CREATIVE LEADER: Camilla Hansteen
DISTRIBUTOR: Alma AS
YEAR OF DEVELOPMENT: 2012
MAIN MATERIAL: paper, glass

PHOTOS: CATHARINA CAPRINO

A Couple of Drops

A Couple of Drops virgin olive oil has a rich velvety flavor, fruity and earthy aroma and a golden color with subtle green tinges. This is reflected by the packaging; white symbolizes the purity of the product, while green references the olive oil itself. The packaging is deliberately understated as the product sells itself and does not require gimmicks and eye-catching imagery.

Traditionally, olive oil is sacred in Greece: a 'divine gift'; important in terms of nutrition, nourishment and ritual. This nutritious 'gold' can be traced back throughout the country's long history, from ancient times, through the Byzantine Empire until now. Olive oil is a vital part of the Greek culinary experience and is always present in a large bottle in the kitchen.

DESIGNER: Beetroot (Greece)
DISTRIBUTOR: A Greek Culture
YEAR OF DEVELOPMENT: 2012
MAIN MATERIAL: screen printing on glass

Design: Beetroot

**A COUPLE
OF DROPS**
of **GREEK
EXTRA
VIRGIN
OLIVE
OIL**

A COUPLE
OF DROPS
of GREEK
EXTRA
VIRGIN
OLIVE
OIL

We welcome you to experience a couple of
drops of extra virgin olive oil, produced
in the Peloponnesian land of Kalamata.
Rich, velvety flavor, fruity and earthy aroma
and a luxurious golden color with a subtle
green tinges...

The extra virgin olive oil as it should be!

agreekculture, 9 Favi Str.,
115 25 Athens, Greece
T. +302106990290, F. +302106990289,
www.agreekculture.gr

OLIVE
OIL

500 ML
PRODUCT OF GREECE

Acidity ≤ 0.5%

A COUPLE
OF DROPS
of GREEK
EXTRA
VIRGIN
OLIVE
OIL

**A COUPLE
OF DROPS**
of **GREEK
EXTRA
VIRGIN
OLIVE
OIL**

Superior category olive oil obtained directly
from olives and solely by mechanical means.

Nutritional Facts per 100ml

	804 Kcal / 3389kj
Energy	0g
Proteins	91.5g
Total Fat	6.5g
– Polyunsaturates	7.7g
– Monounsaturates	13g
– Saturates	0mg
Cholesterol	

Store in a cool place, away from light.

Quality characteristics

Acidity ≤ 0.5%
Petroxides ≤ 20meq O₂/kg
Waxes (ppm) ≤ 250mg/kg
Ultraviolet absorption K232 ≤ 2.50
K270 ≤ 0.22, DK ≤ 0.01

Cold extraction at a temperature below 27°C

Certified by ELOT EN ISO 900:2000
Packed by Sarantos A. Polizois,
24001, Kremmidia, Messinia, Greece

EL 40057

500 ML
PRODUCT OF GREECE

Acidity ≤ 0.5%

5 214000 052029

El Mil del Poaig

Design: CuldeSac

This packaging design was developed to commercialize a millennial olive oil. Due to the market positioning of the client's strategy, it was necessary to develop a special proposal that offers consumers an extraordinary experience beyond the product contained. The two-piece bottle is made out of white porcelain. The oil drips along the spout coming out from the middle of the piece. The bottle color makes the texture, density and color of the oil visible.

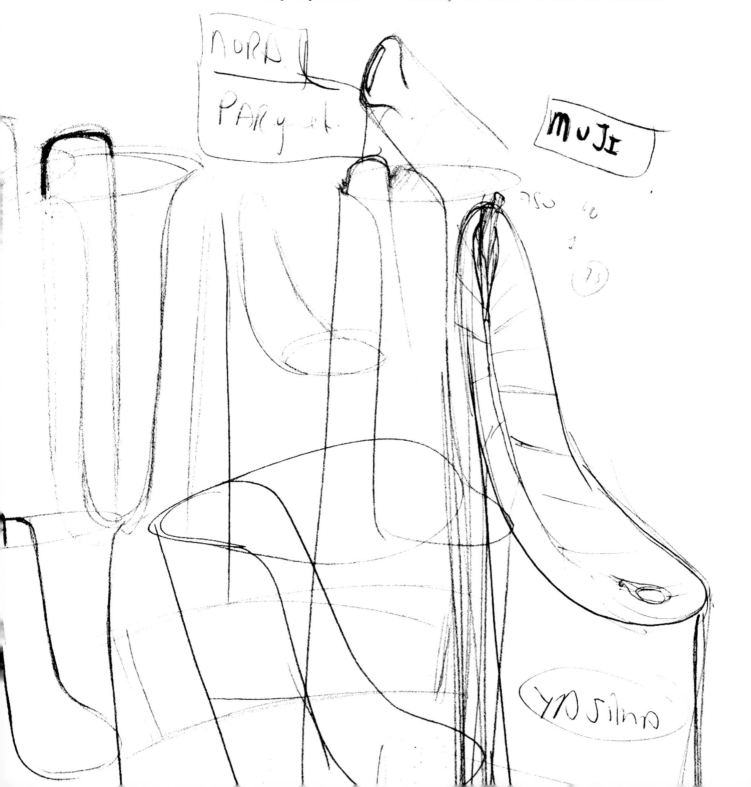

DESIGNER: CuldeSac (Spain)
DISTRIBUTOR: El Poaig
YEAR OF DEVELOPMENT: 2008
MAIN MATERIAL: porcelain

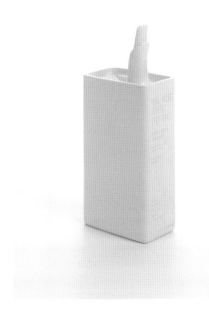

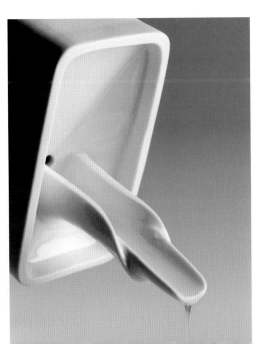

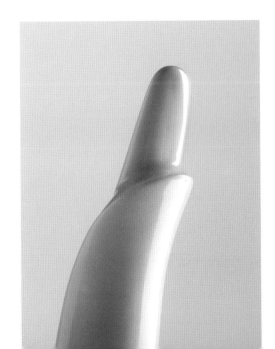

Biodegrade Me

Biodegrade Me is a fast food packaging concept in response to the 2004 documentary Supersize Me in which independent filmmaker Morgan Spurlock consumes fast food for a month. The exterior of the bags are made from recycled pulp paper, providing insulation, whilst the interior is lined with greaseproof grass paper - both are biodegradable. The individual bags are designed to correspond with color branding used for each sandwich at the time of creation. The design and function of the bags is inspired by customer interaction with the packaging - often consumers will rip open their bags to reveal their meal, creating a tray in the process - therefore the bag is created to open out into a comfortable eating station.

DESIGNER: Andrew Millar (United Kingdom)
YEAR OF DEVELOPMENT: 2008
MAIN MATERIAL: recycled pulp paper, grass paper

Design: Andrew Millar

Wiberg Spice Box

Packaging needs to fulfill many
tasks above and beyond just looking
attractive. Of all these tasks the most
intriguing one is the question of how to
access the contents both functionally,
and even more importantly, emotionally;
caviar does not feel right out of a
plastic squeeze bottle à la ketchup.
The designers have tried to create the
right feel for high quality spices from
Wiberg, indeed to help the consumer see,
touch and even savor the precious spices
before adding them to their food. Via
the unique folding chute the user can
make a controlled shake or a delicate
pinch - with the spices in full view.
To conclude, the spice box brings the
user closer to both the spices and the
artistry of professional chefs.

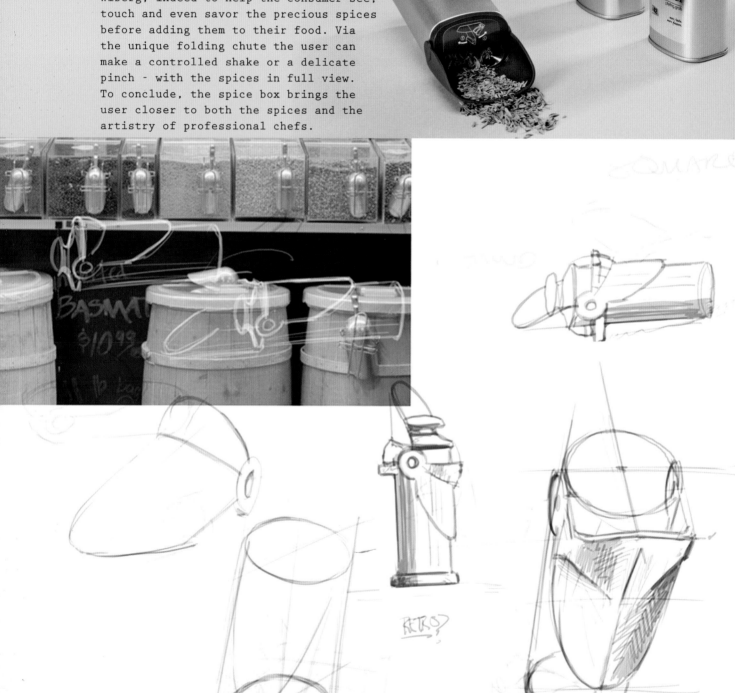

DESIGNER: leon design (Germany)
DISTRIBUTOR: Wiberg
YEAR OF DEVELOPMENT: 2010
MAIN MATERIAL: matt coated tin, plastic

Design: Leon Widdison

Egg Box

The designer's goal was to come up with an innovative egg box that took both the environment and the use of recyclable materials into consideration. The box is made from a single piece of card and the eggs are placed into elliptical holes. Due to the structure, the eggs can be seen without having to open the box. The consumer can get to the eggs by opening the top after removing the label. The label has two functions: to give the consumer information about the product and help to fix the container into position.

DESIGNER: Otília Erdélyi (Hungary)
DISTRIBUTOR: prototype
YEAR OF DEVELOPMENT: 2012
MAIN MATERIAL: cardboard

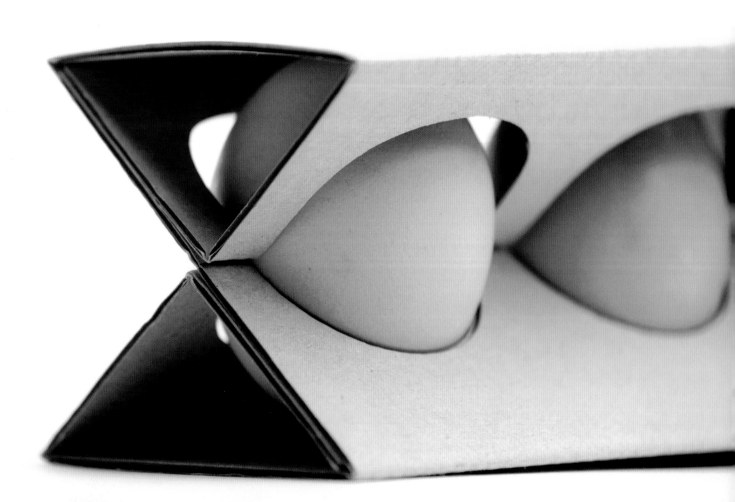

Design: Otília Erdélyi

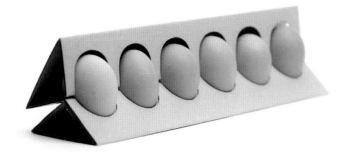

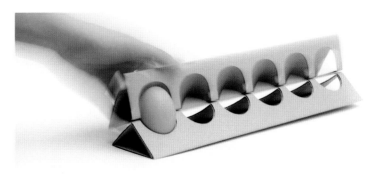

PHOTOS: MILÁN RÁCMOLNÁR, BUDAPEST. PORTRAIT: NÓRA DÉNES, SZOMBATHELY

Pist!

Design: Marie Bergeron

During the designer's bachelor degree in graphic design, she was required to come up with a new way to present a food product. Pistachios were the chosen foodstuffs. Students had to think of a main problem with their desired product, which in this case was the problem of what to do with the shells after the pistachios had been eaten. Rather than putting them on the side, which can be quite untidy, the designer thought of giving her packaging an inbuilt garbage can. If not all of the nuts are consumed at the same time, it is easy to close the package to be consumed later on. The size of the package makes it easy to transport in a backpack or purse. The solution was to propose two sides within the packaging, one for the product itself and the other to be used for garbage.

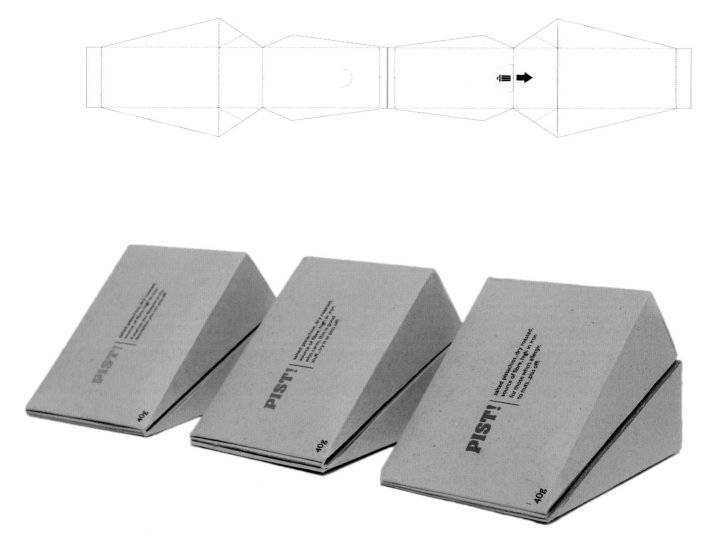

DESIGNER: Marie Bergeron Design Inc./
Marie Bergeron (Canada)
YEAR OF DEVELOPMENT: 2010
MAIN MATERIAL: recycled paper, ink

Pasta La Vista

Pasta La Vista is a brand that covers a wide range of various hand-made macaroni products manufactured in accordance with traditional Italian recipes and using only environmentally friendly products of the highest quality. The designers decided to introduce four characters into the corporate style and package; these are Mario, Francesco, Giovanni and Francesca. Every package depicts one of the characters - an Italian chef in the process of cooking. All the illustrations communicate the character and exclusivity of the trademark. In addition to that, the product in the package can be seen as hair of one of the characters, neatly tucked under the chef's hat.

DESIGNER: Andrew Gorkovenko (Russia)
YEAR OF DEVELOPMENT: 2012
MAIN MATERIAL: cardboard, printing

Beverages

Drink packaging is a discipline at the pinnacle of packaging design, not only must it satisfy the same regulations that apply to food packaging, but it must also be liquid-proof. It is also one of the oldest packaging design disciplines. In the past food and drink were often purchased from markets as single items and not in bulk so it was necessary to package wine and milk accordingly. Coffee and tea as 'solids' are exceptions in this chapter, as were oil and vinegar, as liquid 'foods' in the previous chapter. These examples must meet the requirements of more than one discipline.

The Coca-Cola bottle is a classic example of iconic drink packaging. With its 'female' form - neck, chest, waist and hips - this is one of the most memorable examples of drink packaging, even though the shape has changed somewhat over the years, as has our idea of beauty. Glass bottles are one of the most common types of packaging. Other popular materials include ceramic and pouches - the follow-up to the hoses used in the Antiquity - and various tetrapacks. Standardized bottles are a typical form of drink packaging. However, this form has become so common that it is barely mentioned as a design discipline in this volume. In contrast, the demand for ecological alternatives to plastic bottles is an important consideration in packaging design.

Differently to food packaging, drinks usually stand alone on the shelves so the packaging doesn't need to be stacked. As a result, the projects in this category are much more sculptural in appearance and often inspired by other product forms. Light bulbs, pyramids or a cow's udder are shapes used in drink packaging. The classic milk bottle shape is so iconic that it has also been used to 'hide' unexpected products.

Aside from the actual drink packaging, the products in this category often have a second layer of packaging, giving them a high quality appearance. This is particularly true of alcoholic beverages, and is one of the only differences between packaging for alcoholic and non-alcoholic drinks.

Mount Tea Special Edition

Mount Tea Germany asked designer Elroy Klee to develop a distinctive packaging that would appeal to consumers and stand out from similar products. The shape of the packaging is not only a reference to the pyramid shaped teabags but also to the brand name. The soft colors and geometric shapes decorating the packaging give it an unusual and dynamic appearance; each surface and not just the pyramid shaped package itself has a three dimensional quality. The limited edition packaging can be found in specialty stores.

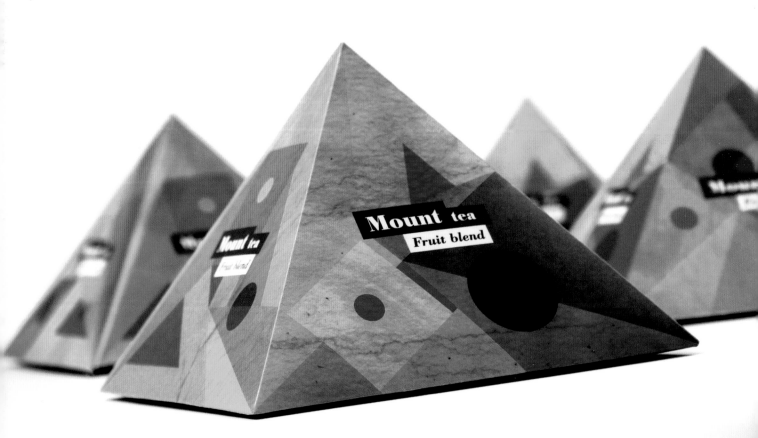

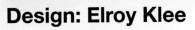

Design: Elroy Klee

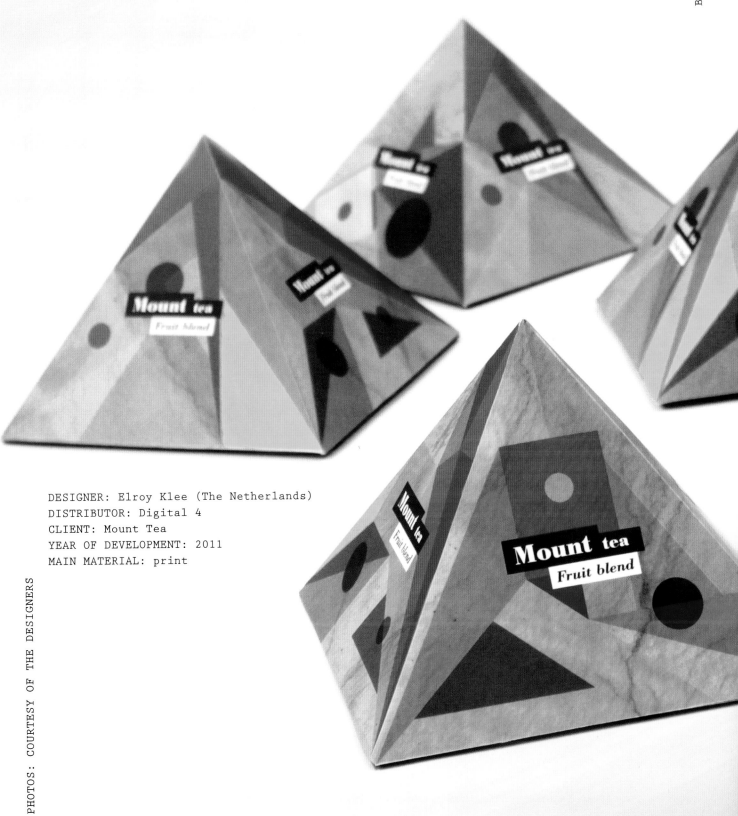

DESIGNER: Elroy Klee (The Netherlands)
DISTRIBUTOR: Digital 4
CLIENT: Mount Tea
YEAR OF DEVELOPMENT: 2011
MAIN MATERIAL: print

Grolsch Icons

Designer Elroy Klee has given the traditional Grolsch beer bottle an exciting twist. Using the distinctive bottle shape, these designs refer to specific events. The black winding design is a roll of film that winds its way up the bottle. The dynamic Zwarte Cross design references the festival of the same name which hosts a range of stunts, motor-cross, music, sports and camping. The idea of linking the Grolsch bottle to specific events adds a personalized touch, making it stand out from the crowd.

Design: Elroy Klee

DESIGNER: Elroy Klee (The Netherlands)
DISTRIBUTOR: Royal Grolsch
YEAR OF DEVELOPMENT: 2011
MAIN MATERIAL: various

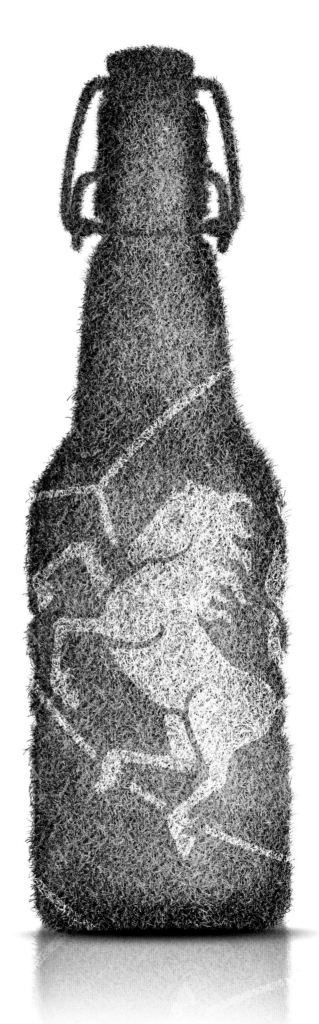

Chinese Tea Box

This design for Jasmine tea reinterprets the traditional tea box - moving away from a decorative metal box to create an appealing package featuring a Chinese character that opens its mouth to give access to the tea inside. This design is fun and interesting, and is intended for re-use once the tea has been used. The eye-catching box is ideal for a wide range of additional uses and will draw attention wherever it is placed around the home.

Design: Carlo Giovani

DESIGNER: Carlo Giovani (Brazil)
DISTRIBUTOR: Carlo Giovani
YEAR OF DEVELOPMENT: 2007
MAIN MATERIAL: paper

PHOTOS: COURTESY OF THE DESIGNERS. PORTRAIT: DIMITRE LIMA, SÃO PAULO

Birdy Juice

Design: Mats Ottdal

The designer got the inspiration from this idea whilst unfolding a juice carton to put in the recycling bin. Birdy Juice is a concept for fruit juice using the form of the juice carton to create wings and feet for bird characters. Its basically a product for kids who can play around with the juice packaging as different kind of birds. It also makes it easier and fun to fold out the packaging before it goes in the recycling.

DESIGNER: Mats Ottdal (Norway)
DISTRIBUTOR: prototype
YEAR OF DEVELOPMENT: 2010
MAIN MATERIAL: carton/tetrapack

Gloji

The idea of the Gloji packaging design is based on three related elements: the brand name, Gloji, the main ingredient, Goji berry, and the slogan "The juice that makes you glow". By using a light bulb-shaped bottle, the ideas of glowing and health are communicated visually.

The packaging represents energy and bright ideas. This innovative light bulb-shaped bottle is very ergonomic. It looks great and fits easily into your hand.

Design: Peter Kao

DESIGNER: Peter Kao / Gloji
DISTRIBUTOR: Gloji
YEAR OF DEVELOPMENT: 2010
MAIN MATERIAL: glass

Blink Champagne

The graphic design of the Blink
Champagne is characterized by its
stripes. This, together with the use
of a small logo on the bottle itself,
defines the brand. The striking design
gives the bottle its strong identity,
making it stand out from other bottles
on display.

DESIGNER: Beetroot (Greece)
DISTRIBUTOR: Blink Wines
YEAR OF DEVELOPMENT: 2008
MAIN MATERIAL: screen printing on glass

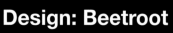

Design: Beetroot

Mixed Emotions

The inspiration behind this project was the idea of selling emotions through a product. The designer selected a mix of a fruit blend and vodka. The concoction is a range of fruit blends that are associated with different emotions, such as love, sadness, happiness, fear and anger. The Mixed Emotions cocktail evokes an emotion and changes the attitude according to the preference. The spiral structure forms two straws that invite the consumer to visualize how the liquids combine as they drink. While the front panel invites the consumer to drink, the back panel depicts phrases to illustrate the type of experience the customer may encounter. Because of its design, the consumers can do whatever they please without worrying about spilling their drink or breaking the bottle.

DESIGNER: Gworkshop Design (Ecuador)
DISTRIBUTOR: Mixed Emotions
YEAR OF DEVELOPMENT: 2010
MAIN MATERIAL: plastic

Design: Gworkshop Design

MIXED EMOTIONS
love+me

LET'S GET HOOKED

vodka+love
STRAWBERRY

20° ALC./VOL | 300ml

MIXED EMOTIONS
fear+me

ENJOY THE MIX

mysterious, eccentric and twisted.

CAUTION:
We are not responsible for the intense night that you
are about to experience. Please drink responsibly.

MIXED EMOTIONS®

MIXED EMOTIONS
happy+me

Soy Mamelle

Soy Mamelle is an innovative concept product for soymilk packaging, created by Kian branding agency. The bottle looks like an udder and presents the first part of the main idea: soymilk is similar to cows' milk. The second part of the message is transmitted via the color code and décor of the packaging, which concentrates on the photogenic quality of the product, communicating an image of naturalness and health. The package is made of recycled PET or glass. It has usable bottle cap and three legs. The Soy Mamelle package has great potential for improvement of brand identity in POS-materials and non-standard trading equipment.

DESIGNER: Kian branding agency, Evgeny Morgalev (Russia)
DISTRIBUTOR: prototype
YEAR OF DEVELOPMENT: 2009
MAIN MATERIAL: recycled PET, glass

Design: Kian branding agency

Ramlösa Premium Bottle

The Ramlösa Premium Bottle is sold in exclusive restaurants, venues and nightclubs. Nine were given the task of designing a new premium bottle in PET. The result is very much a premium product and has been well received both due to its aesthetic appeal and the environmentally positive effects from lower carbon dioxide emissions.

The premium feeling was achieved by creating a bottle that borrows form and shape from the world of old crystal glasses - but with the material that comes from a modern and much less premium world. The contrasts make the result both interesting and beautiful.

DESIGNER: Nine (Sweden)
DISTRIBUTOR: Carlsberg
YEAR OF DEVELOPMENT: 2011
MAIN MATERIAL: PET

Design: Nine

PHOTOS: CHRIS JONKERS, STUDIO BOJO, PORTRAIT: ROBERT ELDRIM, MEDLJUS

GreenBottle

GreenBottle is a British company that produces bottles made out of paper (and a little bit of plastic). The bottles are recyclable and the paper casing is made from recycled wood fiber. GreenBottle originally started making milk bottles but soon began applying its technology to other liquids including wine, juice, oils and homecare products. GreenBottle was invented by Martin Myerscough, who came up with his groundbreaking idea when a landfill manager told him that

plastic bottles are the biggest waste problem in the United Kingdom - almost all end up in landfill where they remain indefinitely. Once a GreenBottle is finished with, the bottle can be ripped apart, the film removed and the paper recycled or composted. This simple but unique packaging solution means the days of heavy, carbon intensive glass, difficult to recycle laminated cartons and oceans of plastic bottles might soon be behind us.

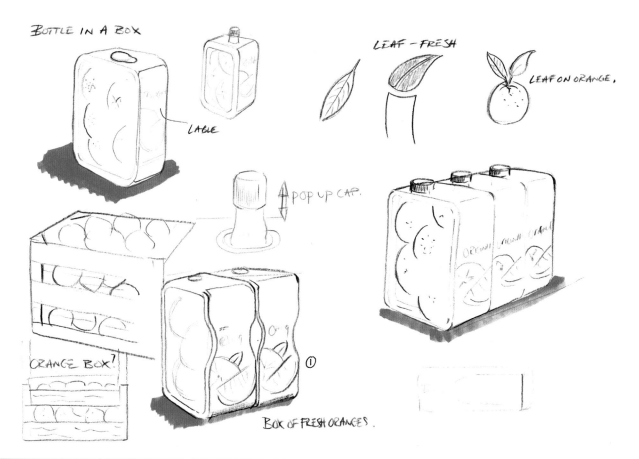

DESIGNER: Martin Myerscough
(United Kingdom)
MANUFACTURER: GreenBottle
YEAR OF DEVELOPMENT: 2005
MAIN MATERIAL: woodfiber, plastic

Design: Martin Myerscough

PHOTOS: A. EVANS, LONDON

Hypnos

Design: Andrea Basile

Hypnos is a product of Longo's winery, made in the province of Salerno, Italy. The production technique involves slowly filtering the wine must through cotton caps, so that Hypnos comes out drop by drop. Longo's winery is a prestigious reality that recovers the century-old tradition of this kind of distillation.

DESIGNER: Andrea Basile /
Basile Advertising (Italy)
DISTRIBUTOR: Vini Longo
YEAR OF DEVELOPMENT: 2011
MAIN MATERIAL: fedrigoni

The Design Business Bottle

This product is a gift, presented to clients. The Design Business Bottle is a two-necked bottle that symbolizes the connection between the company and the client. The two necks are then packaged inside two glasses, one decorated with the words "our business" and the other with "your business".

Design: Irinel Ionescu

And when you put some of your business into our business ... in the end you will be the one drinking from cup.

AMPRO
...endless creativity

Please enjoy it responsibly or not.

our business

is

your business

open here

open here

DESIGNER: Ampro design / Irinel Ionescu
(Romania)
DISTRIBUTOR: Ampro design
YEAR OF DEVELOPMENT: 2010
MAIN MATERIAL: glass

open here

Melo Watermelon Juice

The goal of this design was to create a mouth-watering, intuitive package that immediately attracts consumers and begins to satiate thirst as soon as you lay eyes on it. The designers wanted to bring the product's purity to the forefront while maintaining easy shopability for consumers. Since the type of packaging changes the taste of the product, a sustainable, BPA-free bottle was of the utmost importance. The curvature of the bottle pays homage to the watermelon, with an eye toward ergonomics, and transportability.

DESIGNER: Imagemme (USA)
DISTRIBUTOR: prototype
YEAR OF DEVELOPMENT: 2012
MAIN MATERIAL: glass

Fire Fighter Vodka

The task at hand was to create a striking visual concept for a vodka bottle. The brand name Fire Fighter, the bottle design, and the slogan "Use in case of party" were created by the designer to serve a very clear purpose - to make people want to buy this product. The bright red color and clever use of a shot glass to look like the nozzle of the extinguisher help to make this product stand out from the crowd.

USE IN CASE OF PARTY

DESIGNER: Timur Salikhov (Russia)
DISTRIBUTOR: prototype
YEAR OF DEVELOPMENT: 2012
MAIN MATERIAL: glass

Design: Timur Salikhov

FIRE FIGHTER

VODKA

40% ALC. / 1 LITER

Sexy Tina

This vodka bottle is shaped like a breast and invites the consumer to drink straight from the bottle. The drink itself is a mix of vodka and Irish cream and the shape is of course a reference to the milky drink contained within. The black decoration is inspired by the classic look of a black lacy bra. The packaging is perfectly designed to appeal to its target audience of young men.

DESIGNER: Pavel Gubin (Russia)
DISTRIBUTOR: prototype
YEAR OF DEVELOPMENT: 2009
MAIN MATERIAL: coated or solid white glass, metal cap

Design: Pavel Gubin

milky vodka
35% vol.

LH2O

Design: Rita João, Pedro Ferreira

A mineral water bottle is not only a vessel, but also an interface between liquid and solid, a natural element and cultural product. LH2O reinterprets the shape of water. This innovative bottle protects and maintains the purity of its contents - 33cl of Luso natural mineral water - while seeking to optimize and ease storage, transportation, display, handling and consumption.

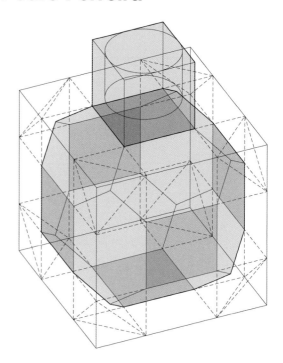

DESIGNER: Pedrita (Portugal)
DISTRIBUTOR: Água de Luso
YEAR OF DEVELOPMENT: 2009
MAIN MATERIAL: PET

LH₂O
Uma experiência
Pedrita
com Água de Luso

LUSO

SOCIEDADE DA ÁGUA DE LUSO, S.A.
3050-902 LUSO - PORTUGAL
Apoio ao cliente 808 20 47 71

Análise conforme boletim nº02/H/2009, do Lab. do INETI / S. Mamede Infesta, de Jan. 2009: pH 5.69 ± 0.13; Sílica (SiO2) 13.1 ± 0.6 mg/L; Mineralização total 46.7 ± 2.0 mg/L; Cálcio 0.74 ± 0.07 mg/L; Fluoreto < 0.08 mg/L; Nitrato 1.68 ± 0.06 mg/L; Sódio 6.9 ± 0.3 mg/L; Magnésio 1.66 ± 0.10 mg/L; Cloreto 9.4 ± 0.3 mg/L; Bicarbonato 11.1

Coca-Cola

The traditional Coca-Cola bottle was first established in 1916 and retains its original form even today. The glass manufacturer Roots Glass Company developed the 19-centimeter bottle with its recognizable fluting. The curving 'female' form is also characteristic of the original design. Inspiration for the design is said to have come from the designer vase by Tiffany's or from the close cut hobble skirt. The shape of the Coca-Cola bottle sets it apart from other drink packaging designs at the time. The tight bottle top and thick glass made the drink more transportable.

DESIGNER: Earl R. Dean (USA)
DISTRIBUTOR: Coca-Cola
YEAR OF DEVELOPMENT: 1915
MAIN MATERIAL: glass

Undercover Pinot Noir

This product is a bottle of wine in disguise. It was developed as a gift from Ampro design to their clients and is a humorous design that stands out for the crowd. The design is intended to highlight the creativity of the designers, and their ability to "think outside the box".

DESIGNER: Ampro design / Irinel Ionescu, Alin Patru (Romania)
DISTRIBUTOR: Ampro design
YEAR OF DEVELOPMENT: 2012
MAIN MATERIAL: glass

Design: Irinel Ionescu

Milk*

A milk bottle?
Yes, we know that you have
never received this kind of
That's why we've packed
finest Pinot Noir in this
bottle of milk.
Enjoy it!

ampro design

Milk*

A milk bottle?
Yes, we know that you have
never received this kind of gift.
That's why we've packed our
finest Pinot Noir in this
bottle of milk.
Enjoy it!

ampro design

*pinot noir

AMPRO DESIGN FARM
UNDERCOVER PINOT NOIR

AMPRO DESIGN FARM
UNDERCOVER PINOT NOIR

JJ Royal

Design: Isabela Rodrigues

JJ Multi Utama Indonesia produces rare, specially picked, premium grade Indonesian coffee beans for the retail market under the brand JJ Royal Coffee; offering the premium quality 100 percent pure Luwak and the best single origin specialty Arabica coffee from Toraja, Mandheling, Kayumas Java Estate, Aceh Gayo, Bali Kintamani, Mt. Bintang

Papua and Flores, along with a range of specially selected unique highland Robusta. The designers proudly made the brand packing JJ Royal, which produces the purest grains of Indonesia. The minimalistic design uses geometric and organic forms, resulting in a clear, pure and modern container.

DESIGNER: Isabela Rodrigues / Sweety Branding Studio (Brazil)
DISTRIBUTOR: JJ Royal
YEAR OF DEVELOPMENT: 2012
MAIN MATERIAL: tetrapack, polycarbonate, cardboard

Juicy

Design: Krešimir Miloloža

This experimental project evolved from analysis of color potential in packaging design. The intention was to give the packaging a stronger promotional function, making it more eye-catching. Visual unification, the use of color and images created uninterrupted continuous surface of 56 centimeters in length. That is truly impossible not to notice in the supermarket.

DESIGNER: Krešimir Miloloža (Croatia)
AGENCY: DNA
DISTRIBUTOR: prototype
YEAR OF DEVELOPMENT: 2009
MAIN MATERIAL: tetrapack

CHERRY · STRAWBERRY · APRICOT · ORANGE · PINEAPPLE · APPLE · BLUEBERRY · BLACK CURRANT

Tea Tube

Design: Allen Lin and Rex Hsieh

This product is called Tea Tube; the test tube is a symbol for the process of experimenting and exploring the unknown world. Most packages keep tea leaves in dark containers, making it hard to tell the flavor. The designers solve this issue by using PET tubes. The transparent tube design balances the dark and heavy appearance of the tea leaves. The tube also serves as a quirky decoration for any desk or room.

DESIGNER: Rex Hsieh and Allen Lin / Tea Smile (Taiwan)
DISTRIBUTOR: Tea Smile
YEAR OF DEVELOPMENT: 2011
MAIN MATERIAL: paper, PET tubes

Gordon's – Ten Green Bottles

Ten Green Bottles is a novel collaboration between two iconic British brands, Gordon's and Conran. Taking inspiration from Sir Terence Conran's textile archive, the team created ten patterns that brought a fresh twist to the classic green bottle. The patterns feature on two limited edition ranges of Gordon's. One million special bottles with tactile fabric labels replaced the standard bottles on shop shelves - a bold move for a 250-year-old market leader. Additionally, 200 premium bottles with hand-stitched cotton wraps and presentation cases were available at Selfridges. Each pattern incorporates a number from one to ten - a nod to the British rhyme that gave the project its name.

DESIGNER: Emma Booty / Conran Studio (United Kingdom)
DISTRIBUTOR: Diageo
YEAR OF DEVELOPMENT: 2012
MAIN MATERIAL: cotton

Design: Emma Booty

Got Milk

Design: Isabela Rodrigues

Got Milk is a brand of flavored milk, and this project involved new branding for the US market. The designers were asked to develop packaging for all product lines. This particular design is for the Cocoa line, the company's most important product, making up around 50 percent of its sales. The design brings a new modernity to the brand, giving it a fresh new identity. The white lettering of the word milk references the product in its purest form, while the brown background is a clear indicator of the cocoa flavor.

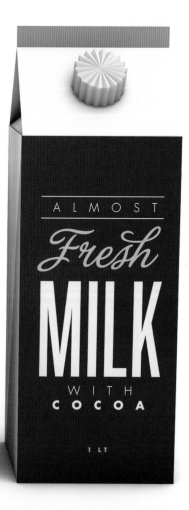

DESIGNER: Isabela Rodrigues / Sweety Branding Studio (Brazil)
YEAR OF DEVELOPMENT: 2012
MAIN MATERIAL: tetrapack

Cavallum

Cavallum is a box of wine that trans-
forms into a lamp. Originally created
as a corporate gift for Hera Holding,
Cavallum is made of recycled carton and
wood from controlled reforestation projects. At that time, Hera, a waste management firm based in Barcelona, asked
Tati Guimarães for a gift that would
communicate a powerful ecological
message.

DESIGNER: Tati Guimarães (Spain)
DISTRIBUTOR: Ciclus
CLIENT: Hera Holding
YEAR OF DEVELOPMENT: 2008
MAIN MATERIAL: 100% recycled cardboard,
certified wood

Per obrir la capsa, pressioneu
Para abrir la caja, presionar
AQUÍ

Design: Tati Guimarães

PHOTOS: LUIZ SIMÕES. PORTRAIT: PACO BOFARULL

Kavalan Whisky Event Packaging

Due to the company's desire to include a 50 ml gift bottle with each 700 ml bottle of whiskey, the packaging needed to be redesigned to be able to hold and display both bottles at once in order to attract customer attention. A six-sided design, with wood accents, along with the brilliant golden colored liquor, was chosen to set it apart from other products on the market. This package design allowed the customers to easily realize the quality of the contents without the need to open the package.

DESIGNER: Rex Hsieh / HJCZ Design Studio (Taiwan)
YEAR OF DEVELOPMENT: 2012
DISTRIBUTOR: King Car Food Industrial Co. LTD
MAIN MATERIAL: paper

Design: Rex Hsieh

Capri-Sonne / Capri-Sun

The classic Capri-Sun pouch with straw is the lightest of all beverage packaging: 4.05 grams of material are enough to hold 200 ml of Capri-Sun effectively and safely. The foil of the pouch comprises PET/PE and aluminum. The plastic gives the product the stability and hygienic safety that a beverage packaging needs. The ultra-thin layer of aluminum protects the sensitive contents from the effects of oxidation and light. One of the requests most often expressed by Capri-Sun consumers was the wish for a larger and resealable pouch. Capri-Sun fulfilled this desire by developing the Spouted Pouch. It was brought to market in 2007 as a 330 ml version in Germany and the UK and soon won the hearts of the Capri-Sun consumers. In the meantime this Capri-Sun variant is offered successfully in more than 30 countries worldwide. Additionally, a 250 ml Spouted Pouch is the perfect packaging for the first organic Capri-Sun launched in 2011 in Germany, the Bio-Schorly.

Design: Rudolf Wild

DESIGNER: Rudolf Wild (Germany)
DISTRIBUTOR: Deutsche SiSi-Werke
Betriebs GmbH
YEAR OF DEVELOPMENT: 1969
MAIN MATERIAL: thin foil

Cubis1

Design: Jonas Lundin, Erik Nilsson

Cubis1 is an innovative packaging solution for the beverage industry. It combines the logistical benefits of paper packaging with user friendliness and appeal of plastic bottles. The patented beverage container brings a number of benefits to producers, distributors and consumers. It reduces costs as well as carbon emissions by improved utilization of space during transportation and storage. A higher level of protection against contamination through the sealed drinking spout. The bottles are easier to stack, increasing shelf space and simplifying handling. The design is also eye-catching, facilitating the market introduction of new beverage products.

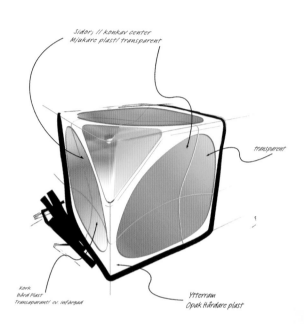

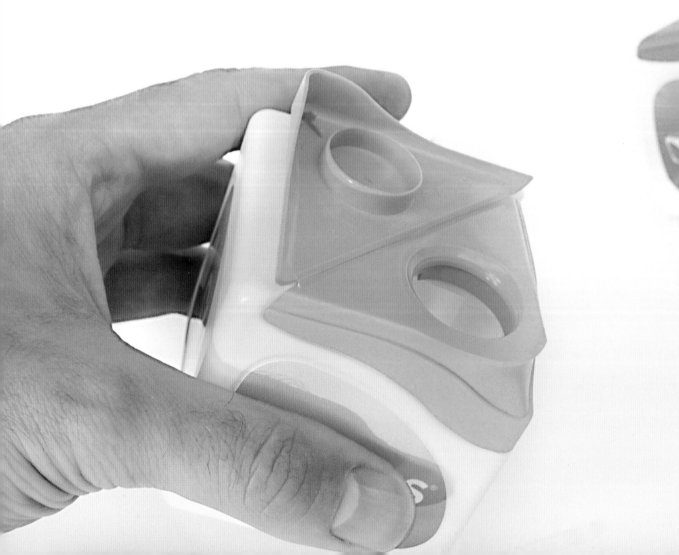

DESIGNER: Jonas Lundin / Erik Nilsson (Sweden)
DISTRIBUTOR: Formteknik
YEAR OF DEVELOPMENT: 2009
MAIN MATERIAL: plastic

Mr Brown Coffee Event Packaging

Mr. Brown coffee is a long time producer of canned coffee in the Taiwan market. Following recent global trends, the brand decided to enter the cafe and gourmet coffee market. In order to attract the growing number of coffee lovers to the Mr. Brown brand, the company decided to release additional products and update their designs to appeal to the tastes of younger consumers. The design is meant to invoke a sense of a sense of a rich and complex coffee flavor that leaves a lasting impression with customers.

DESIGNER: Rex Hsieh / HJCZ Design Studio (Taiwan)
DISTRIBUTOR: King Car Food Industrial Co. LTD.
YEAR OF DEVELOPMENT: 2012
MAIN MATERIAL: paper

Design: Rex Hsieh

Leuven Beer

Design: Wonchan Lee

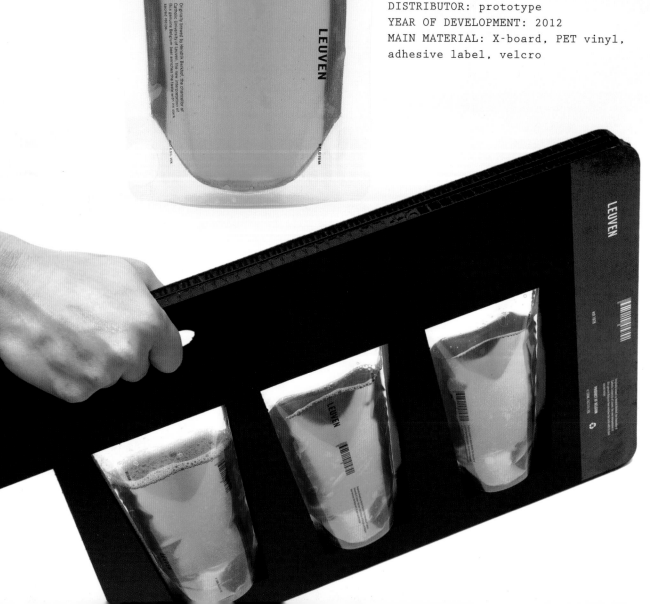

Belgium. Premium. Beer. Those are the three words the designer had to keep in mind while designing the range. The aim was to differentiate the brand and packaging from other market competitors as well as clearly communicate and maintain its identity. With the under-stated color palette throughout the design, the color of the beer creates a great contrast and stands out. Not only is the material used in the package lighter, but also more economical than widely used glass. It therefore has advantages in terms of both cost and shipping.

DESIGNER: Wonchan Lee (Australia)
DISTRIBUTOR: prototype
YEAR OF DEVELOPMENT: 2012
MAIN MATERIAL: X-board, PET vinyl, adhesive label, velcro

TripTea

At the heart of brand communication is the idea of traveling to exotic countries of the world, which gives us TripTea tea, and opens up a new world of flavor with each new package. The designers wanted to show the beauty, depth and fullness of the tea only. Therefore, packaging was decorated with landscape scenes from where it was picked and produced. All landscapes are handmade, using the tea variety contained in the package. This conveys an exotic image of the country as well as the richness of flavors and nuances of the product itself. The designers have managed to capture the spirit of adventure and the flavor of traveling, showing an exotic and unforgettable world of tea in all its colors.

DESIGNER: Andrew Gorkovenko (Russia)
YEAR OF DEVELOPMENT: 2012
MAIN MATERIAL: tea, card

Minta

DESIGNER: Constantine Kobernik / DDC Creative Lab (Russia)
DISTRIBUTOR: BevMarketing Group Company, Inc.
YEAR OF DEVELOPMENT: 2012
MAIN MATERIAL: glass, plastic, aluminum

Minta is a 100 percent naturally sweetened and flavored beverage that provides a crisp, bubbly taste with its unique mint flavor. The project included creation of trademark logo, packaging and label design as well as its adaptation for the product range (Minta Original and Minta Diet in glass bottle, plastic bottle and slim can), shrink wrap multipack design. The green colored bottle was inspired by a water drop, with an additional embossing effect that has made its surface tactile and pleasant to touch. The agency applied a no-label effect, using minimal neck label instead of traditional face label effect, which aimed to emphasize Minta among its competitive range. The simple and understandable design idea communicates the purity and freshness of the drink.

In/Fusion

Design: Billie Jean

In/Fusion, the next generation of French tisane, is a blast of freshness and well being taking over the city. A 100 percent organic blend of rare plants, grown in France and charged with the natural healing virtues, associated with fruit juice and pure water. In/Fusion takes the consumer on a tour of cities, pioneering a new lifestyle in urban environments: nomadic, hedonistic and in fusion with nature.

DESIGNER: Billie Jean (United Kingdom)
DISTRIBUTOR: Drinkyz - alternative food and beverage
YEAR OF DEVELOPMENT: 2012
MAIN MATERIAL: tetrapack

Freezing Cold Tea

This package is designed for cold-brewed tea bags, which are immersed in cold water and mainly consumed during summer. Long rectangular tea bags have been used here, instead of square shaped tea bags, allowing consumers to easily drop the bag into or take out of PET water bottles, and use them repeatedly. The designers' idea was inspired by the form of an ice flake. The product is designed to evoke the feeling of coldness. Consumers can see the ice flake on the outer surface. No glue was used in the production of the product. The latch design makes the structure strong, beautiful, and environmentally-friendly.

DESIGNER: Joyce Lin and Allen Lin / Tea Smile (Taiwan)
DISTRIBUTOR: Tea Smile
YEAR OF DEVELOPMENT: 2012
MAIN MATERIAL: paper, long rectangular tea bags

Design: Allen Lin and Joyce Lin

PHOTOS: ARRON CHANG, SPACIOUS CHENG

Body Care

As with food and beverage packaging, body care products must also display the product ingredients. The aesthetic appearance is of more importance in this category as it has a stronger influence on purchasing decisions. The previous two product types provide nourishment, while this category is concerned with improving appearance - so the product itself must also be beautiful. The packaging reveals and describes the function of the product - romantic soap packaging communicates the nature of the product to the consumer, as does a 'sporty' perfume bottle or an elegant container made of natural materials. The package is the message.

There is a huge variety of cut glass 'flakons' (the French word for perfume bottle) with narrow necks on the market, these alone could fill an entire book. The products included in this volume are exemplary; no conceivable design is too complicated. The contents appeal to one sense, smell, while optically, the products in this category differ very little from each other. Drink packaging is often sculptural in appearance, but body care bottles in comparison are almost miniature works of art - sometimes prefigured and sometimes abstract. These often continue to be functional even after they are empty, often serving as ornaments. Here the packaging itself is valuable and often expensive to produce, comparable in terms of quality to a vase or ornament. Other products in this category have to follow this trend if they want to compete in the same field or meet the same standards as luxury products.

CARE

Sofi Bath Bombs

Sofi is a small family-run business that produces organic handmade cosmetics. The packaging design emphasizes the manual production and quality of the resources as well as of the final products. Popular Bruketa&Zinic OM created the design for the line of products so that each of them is differentiated from the rest, by adding a separate initial of its name. Popular Bruketa&Zinic OM have tried to add a particular handmade touch to the typography, which is a characteristic of the entire range of Sofi organic products.

DESIGNER: Popular Bruketa & Zinic OM (Croatia)
DISTRIBUTOR: Sofi
YEAR OF DEVELOPMENT: 2012
MAIN MATERIAL: Paperboard, gold foil, metal lid, cardboard

Choco Loco
CL

Poslastica za
vašu kožu :)

Lavanda
L

Čarobna umirujuća
kupka

Pure Love
PL

NAJLEPŠI NAČIN DA NEKOM
IZJAVITE LJUBAV :D

Deep Blue
B

MORSKI TALASI
V VAŠOJ KADI

Vanila
V

UŽIVAJTE, UŽIVAJTE
I SAMO UŽIVAJTE!

Codizia

Design: Nacho Lavernia and Alberto Cienfuegos

Codizia is a fragrance, developed for women who look for a quality and premium product, but at a much lower price than the top range perfumes. The bottle communicates elegance, personality and sophistication. With its rounded shapes, the gold-finished glass, and the two curved white surfaces produce a light and reflection effect. The package has a graphic design that refers to the shapes and colors of the bottle. It is distributed exclusively at Mercadona chain of supermarkets.

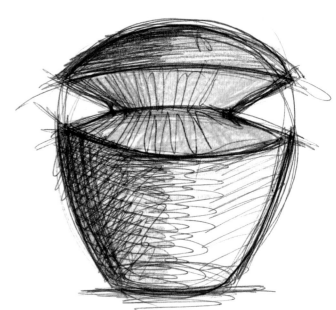

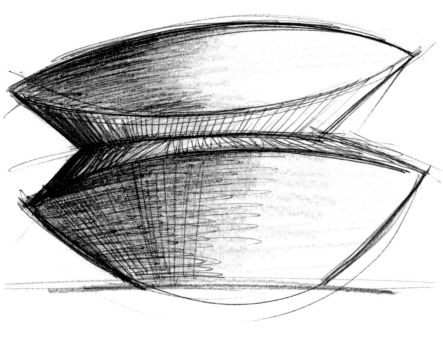

DESIGNER: Lavernia & Cienfuegos Diseño (Spain)
DISTRIBUTOR: RNB Laboratorios for Mercadona
YEAR OF DEVELOPMENT: 2008
MAIN MATERIAL: glass, plastic

PHOTOS: JAVIER CASTARNARDO, VALENCIA, PORTRAIT: ALBERTO CIENFUEGOS, VALENCIA

Bamboo, Cherry and Coconut

Although the colorful, happy image of Fruits & Passion is still present, the cherry, bamboo and coconut packaging strives to convey a more minimalist approach with a generous use of white space. This look is turning heads in-store, where the artistic nature of the photography captures all the originality of this elegant and sophisticated brand.

DESIGNER: Anne-Marie Clermont / lg2boutique (Canada)
CLIENT: Brigitte Roy, Séverine Mathé - Fruits & Passion
YEAR OF DEVELOPMENT: 2011
MAIN MATERIAL: glass, paper

Design: Anne-Marie Clermont

Zen

The Zen packaging concept is the synthesis of organic shape and perfume bottle. The organic shape dominates the design solution and the glass serves a functional purpose - to observe the level of the remaining perfume. Tactile sensations are very important. The smoothness of the glass fragments make the texture and density of the plastic packaging appear and feel very natural, just like a real stone, bamboo or a shell. The main objective of the packaging was to highlight the natural character of this line of perfumes and is fully consistent with the idea of Zen - calm, contemplative and naturally beautiful.

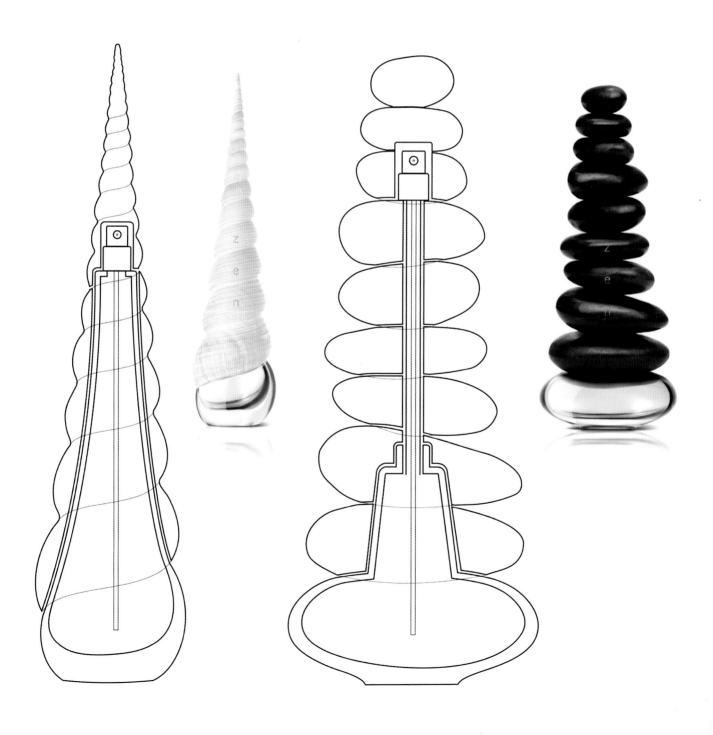

Design: Igor Mitin

DESIGNER: Igor Mitin (Australia)
YEAR OF DEVELOPMENT: 2011
MAIN MATERIAL: plastic, glass

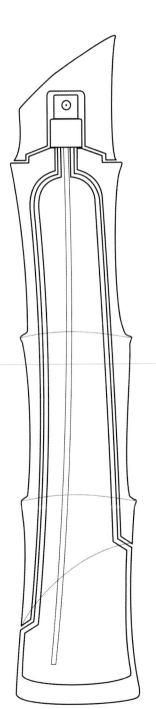

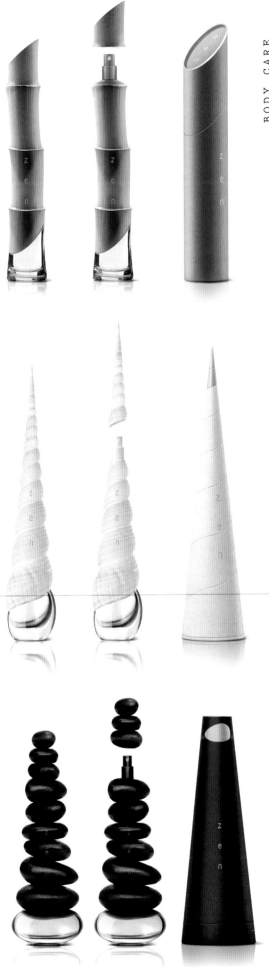

Féerie
Van Cleef & Arpels

Féerie is a fragrance line that embodies
the imaginative values of the luxurious
Van Cleef & Arpels jewelry: precious,
feminine, poetic, and ingenious. The
Féerie bottle, bearing an iconic fairy,
represents the first interpretation of
a new brand concept: jewel perfumes.
The bottle, faceted like a precious
stone, illuminates the mystery of the
luxurious Van Cleef & Arpels perfumery.
The package's most distinguished feature
is its unexpected oversized silver
cap bearing an iconic fairy resting
delicately in an impish pose atop a
moonflower. This sensitive and poetic
character symbolizes the perfume's
magical muse.

Design: Eric Douane

DESIGNER: Eric Douane - Brandimage Paris (France)
DISTRIBUTOR: Van Cleef & Arpels
YEAR OF DEVELOPMENT: 2008
MAIN MATERIAL: glass bottle, fairy cap in
galvanized zamac

Vivid Perfume Package

This perfume packaging was developed
during Harmony Ho's studies with
Professor Randall Sexton at San Jose
State University. The objective was to
package a classmate's personality into
a perfume. Using this inspiration, the
designer came up with a solution of
shiny silver paper and decorated with
a bright pink.

DESIGNER: Harmony Ho (USA)
YEAR OF DEVELOPMENT: 2009
MAIN MATERIAL: paper, glass

Design: Harmony Ho

Pureology

Design: Robert Bergman

The Pureology bottle takes the form of a sensuously curved and innovative multi-functional design - one sits on its cap the other on its base - that is manufactured from a single mold. The creative brief for Pureology presented three main challenges: Firstly, to create a beautifully organic shape; secondly, to create a brand cool enough to be sold at Colette in Paris; and thirdly, to create a package that maximizes the brand's high 'eco values'.

DESIGNER: Bergman Associates Mpakt / Robert Bergman (USA)
DISTRIBUTOR: L'Oreal
YEAR OF DEVELOPMENT: 2012
MAIN MATERIAL: bottle made with 50 percent recycled materials

PHOTOS: COURTESY OF THE DESIGNERS, PORTRAIT: DEREK BLANKS

Sonrisa

Challenged with capturing the essence of Latino culture while translating it for an American audience the designer targeted artistic Latino/American males interested in chic and modern boutique fragrances. It was important to create a memorable package that conveyed bold style and sophistication. The designer was inspired by the exuberance and precision that Latin percussion music embodies, especially the metal cabasa which was created by Martin Cohen, founder of Latin percussion.

DESIGNER: Stephen Edmond (USA)
DISTRIBUTOR: Stephen Edmond
YEAR OF DEVELOPMENT: 2011
MAIN MATERIAL: wood, plastic, metal, cardboard, paper

PHOTOS: COURTESY OF THE DESIGNERS; PORTRAIT: DEREK BLANKS, ATLANTA

Design: Stephen Edmond

Deux Toiles Hotel Bathroom Amenities

Deux Toiles is a high-end bathroom amenity range for The Cullen, a boutique hotel located in Melbourne, Australia, and was inspired by contemporary artist Adam Cullen. The designer attempted to come up with a concept for a bathroom amenity range that also has an individual identity to attract customers as well as provide them with something to remember the hotel by. The packaging is white with elegant black lettering; simple but functional.

DESIGNER: Wonchan Lee (Australia)
DISTRIBUTOR: prototype
YEAR OF DEVELOPMENT: 2012
MAIN MATERIAL: paper, glass, adhesive labels

Design: Wonchan Lee

Honeymoon Fragrance

Honeymoon Fragrance is a product that is light and refreshing, like a cup of tea. Inside this sea urchin shell is an organic perfume made from grapefruit and basil essential oils. This bottle is refillable, so it can be used over and over. It is packaged in a wooden box, decorated with a satin photograph, and padded with slices of exfoliating loofah sponges. It includes an atomizer pump for tabletop use. This fragrance is 100 percent natural. It is made from plant-based oils and contains no alcohol or chemicals.

DESIGNER: Stephanie Simek (USA)
DISTRIBUTOR: Stephanie Simek
YEAR OF DEVELOPMENT: 2010
MAIN MATERIAL: sea urchin shell, wood, glass, loofah sponges

Design: Stephanie Simek

Heidelberger Organic Body Care

Heidelberger naturkosmetik is a new brand of high-quality natural cosmetics for kids. The certified products contain natural ingredients from controlled organic cultivation. With funny ideas and stories about Karo the Cat and an innovative packaging solution, the cosmetics line aims to convey the fun aspects of natural body care to its young target group. The design concept also allows for a valuable educational alternative use of the packaging: children may play with boxes, using them to build towers and bridges of a knight's castle.

Design: Heidi Fleig-Golks

DESIGNER: Heidi Fleig-Golks /
grafik und form (Germany)
DISTRIBUTOR: Tinti GmbH & Co. KG
YEAR OF DEVELOPMENT: 2011
MAIN MATERIAL: paper

PHOTOS: NICO RADEMACHER, PORTRAIT: ANNA LOGUE

Ego

Design: Nacho Lavernia and Alberto Cienfuegos

Ego aims to connect with a modern audience of sophisticated people who are concerned about their appearance. The faceted glass pack has been painted in matte silver, so that the volume of the piece is solid and clearly defined. Ego uses a visual language which is direct and at the same time refined. The logo starts with a Didot typeface in which the characteristics of the letter 'g' have been enlarged so that in context three letters together form a single entity with more personality. It is distributed exclusively at the Mercadona chain of supermarkets.

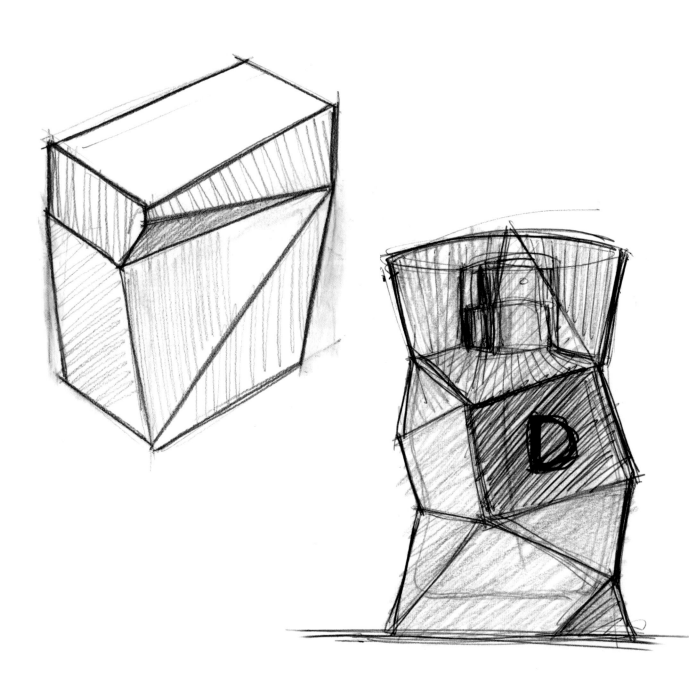

DESIGNER: Lavernia & Cienfuegos Diseño (Spain)
DISTRIBUTOR: RNB Laboratorios for Mercadona
YEAR OF DEVELOPMENT: 2010
MAIN MATERIAL: glass, plastic

PHOTOS: ENRIC PÉREZ, VALENCIA. PORTRAIT: ALBERTO CIENFUEGOS, VALENCIA

Shu Uemura

Design: Robert Bergman

The concept idea behind this design was
to combine beauty with art and Japanese
traditions to create an exclusive and
minimalistic packaging solution that
respects Shu Uemura history. Bergman
Associates worked together with the
French designer Christophe Pillet on
the silhouettes of the bottles of
shampoo and masques products.

DESIGNER: Bergman Associates Mpakt /
Robert Bergman (USA)
DISTRIBUTOR: Shu Uemura
YEAR OF DEVELOPMENT: 2011
MAIN MATERIAL: PET

DEPSEA
SMOOTHING
FOUNDATION
ESSENTIAL HAIR PREP
5FLOZ/150ml

SILK OF
CAMELLIA
SMOOTHING FLUID
1.7 FL OZ/50ml

IRONDES
PROTE
THERMAL S
5FLOZ/1

SHU UEMURA
ART OF HAIR.

You Smell

You Smell started as the student design project of Megan Cummins. The vintage-inspired bath and beauty products focus on elegant typography, ornate flourishes, and classy woodcut-illustrations. Muted candy colors make them stand out while enticing you to smell their delicious scents. Every aspect is something to talk about, creating an emotional connection through every detail - from the design, to the meticulously crafted romance copy that provides just the right balance of wit and charm. The goal of You Smell is to create conversation starters by bringing together luxury and personality in one visually and fragrantly scrumptious package.

DESIGNER: Megan Cummins, Aaron Heth (USA)
DISTRIBUTOR: You Smell, LLC
YEAR OF DEVELOPMENT: 2012
MAIN MATERIAL: natural, recycled papers, biodegradable muslin bags

Design:
Megan Cummins, Aaron Heth

Let's face it: people who smell good, and sometimes this can be a daunting task. Allow us to help. You Smell® has handcrafted you the finest soap, rich in softening shea butter and moisturizing olive oil. This all-natural soap will cleanse the body and ease the soul. Just lather and wash your way to happiness.

Thanks to us!

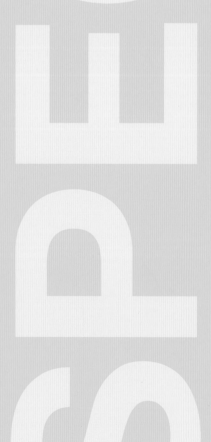

Special

This chapter includes a wide range of hardware products, with a focus on the home and workplace. In contrast to food, drink and body care products, projects included in this chapter - except for the medicines - are subject to fewer regulations. The variety of materials and shapes displayed here is also huge. Some of the projects consider the presentation of the product when it displayed on a shelf or hanging in a shop. This simplifies the task of displaying the product but does confine it to a specific category. Many of the examples in this volume are designed as a packaging system, optimizing the use of available storage space.

A playful approach to the utilization of prefigured forms is also apparent here, packages often hide a different product to what one would expect. The element of surprise is a much-loved sales tactic: paperclips in a sardine tin, a cleaning product that draws attention to its own strength with a dumbbell-shaped container, a designer who emphasis how 'hot' his company is by packaging his portfolio in what appears to be a salsa-dip container, and an apparently solid wooden block that actually houses a valuable ring. Every conceivable material has been used: metal, glass, wood, plastic, paper, card, and many besides.

Paper was first used as a packaging material as far back as 1035, at a time when it was still a very valuable commodity, a Persian traveler visiting markets in Cairo noted that vegetables, spices and hardware were wrapped in paper for the customers after they were sold. The paper and card packages in this volume, however, strive to draw attention to their own ecological aspects; even the colors used are selected to serve this purpose. Customers also associate such environmentally friendly packaging with an environmentally friendly product.

The unpacking process is celebrated as part of the purchasing experience; packaging is no longer just a protective shell or a tool, it extends beyond the functional to really become part of the product itself.

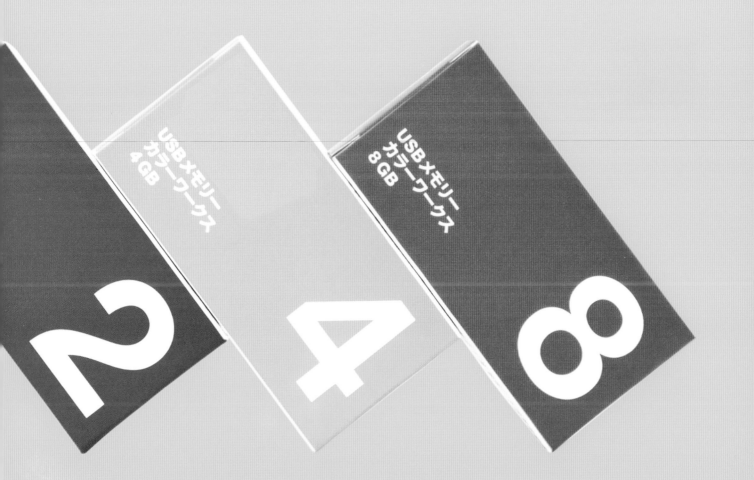

Sardine Paper Clips

Packed in a cool reusable tin, these paper clips can keep an ocean of pages neat and organized. These fish-shaped paperclips are ideal for home, school and everyday office needs. The packaging of course also has an element of surprise, as what is inside is not what is advertised on the outside. This brings an element of fun to a product that is normally only considered as an essential office tool.

PHOTOS: DAN LEV

DESIGNER: Ototo (Israel)
YEAR OF DEVELOPMENT: 2011
MAIN MATERIAL: tin, plastic-coated metal

Sun Candle

Design: Oleg Ivanov

Natural Sun Candles are a new product from Riga Soap Manufacture. The task was to develop two types of candle of the same size and with similar packaging designs. The main rule was to use only natural materials - no plastic, no glue. The designers chose unbleached recyclable cardboard with two-color printing. In order to create something special there are windows cut out of both styles of box through which part of the booklet can be seen, lying inside on the top of the candle. Thus the white paper booklet serves as 'teeth' for the sun and as 'petals' for the flowers. The designers also use special stamps to label each sort of candle. Unusual solutions make these boxes eye-catching and cost effective.

DESIGNER: Oleg Ivanov /
Open Union of Packaging Designers (Latvia)
DISTRIBUTOR: Riga Soap Manufacture
YEAR OF DEVELOPMENT: 2012
MAIN MATERIAL: unbleached recyclable cardboard

"This" Toothbrush

The Miswak is a tooth-cleaning twig used mainly in the Middle East, Pakistan and India. Traditionally, the top is bitten off with every use to reveal soft bristles similar to that of a tooth-brush. The "This" toothbrush aims to repackage and promote the Miswak as an organic, biodegradable, portable, more beneficial substitute for toothpaste and a toothbrush. The carrying case is a transparent tube with a cigar-cutter-like cap. "This" toothbrush started off as a student project for a Masters in Design Entrepreneurship program at the School of Visual Arts, but after receiving overwhelming interest from several communities and individuals, it's finally becoming a reality.

DESIGNER: Leen Sadder (USA)
DISTRIBUTOR: prototype
YEAR OF DEVELOPMENT: 2011
MAIN MATERIAL: miswak

Design: Leen Sadder

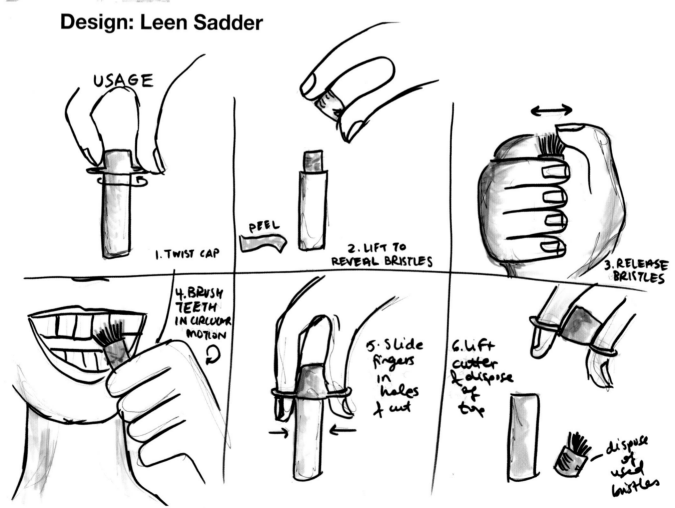

USAGE

1. TWIST CAP

PEEL

2. LIFT TO REVEAL BRISTLES

3. RELEASE BRISTLES

4. BRUSH TEETH IN CIRCULAR MOTION

5. Slide fingers in holes & cut

6. Lift cutter & dispose of top

— dispose of used bristles

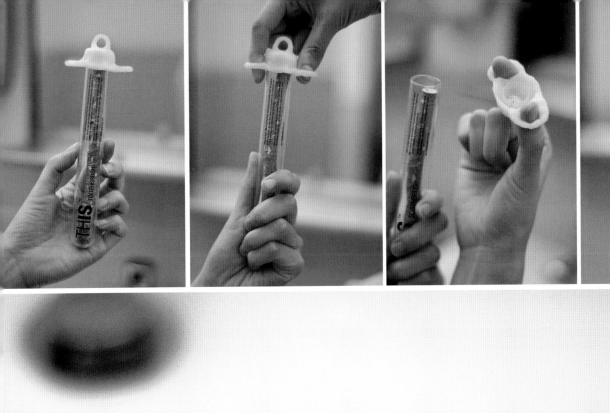

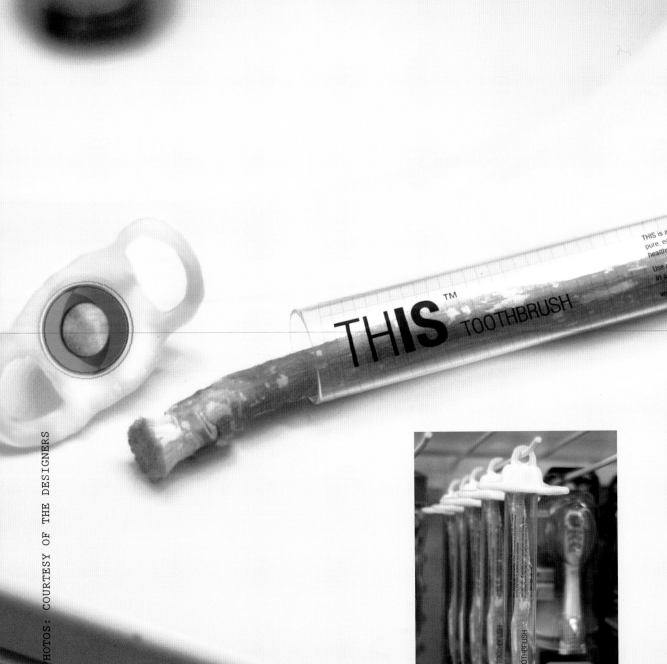

THIS™ TOOTHBRUSH

THIS is a teeth-cleaning twig from the
pure, easy to use, and portable. It ha
healthy alternative to toothbrush an

Use cap to slice off seal and reve
in a circular motion. Use cap to

www.thistoothbrush.com

Bambum

Design: Tati Guimarães

The concept was to design a Christmas gift that would highlight the subject of sustainability. The object designed was a playful object that, when assembled, becomes a Christmas tree and after Christmas it can be reused. The title on the box "Preserve Christmas" has a double meaning: to preserve the environment and to preserve the Christmas tradition. The object is made of bamboo wood and the pack uses the minimum material and processes. The assembly instructions are printed inside the box to save paper.

DESIGNER: Tati Guimarães (Spain)
DISTRIBUTOR: Ciclus
YEAR OF DEVELOPMENT: 2010
MAIN MATERIAL: bamboo, recycled cardboard

PHOTOS: LUIZ SIMÕES, PORTRAIT: PACO BOFARULL

Jewelry Box Klotz

This packaging is made of six identical oiled wooden cubes. A leathern hinge provides the opening function and a paper loop is used to keep the box closed. A logo can easily be printed on it. Klotz not only protects the jewelry inside but also displays it beautifully. The entire packaging is made out of nature material and is 100 percent biodegradable. The boxes are not immediately recognizable as jewelry packaging and it is not clear on which side the box will open.

DESIGNER: Gerlinde Gruber Packaging Design (Austria)
DISTRIBUTOR: Gerlinde Gruber
YEAR OF DEVELOPMENT: 2010
MAIN MATERIAL: nut wood, leather, paper

Design: Gerlinde Gruber

PHOTOS: STEPHAN FRIESINGER, GRAZ

Herokid Magic Box

Herokid is a clothing brand created by Robert Roman. The main reference for this brand and the people who compose it is the culture of skateboarding and street art from the streets of Barcelona. The concept for this package was to create a box that can be a functional t-shirt package as well as a decorative and promotional device. The Herokid logo served as inspiration to design a package in corrugated card that needs no adhesive for assembling. There's also a small version which can be downloaded from the internet for those who want to make one themselves.

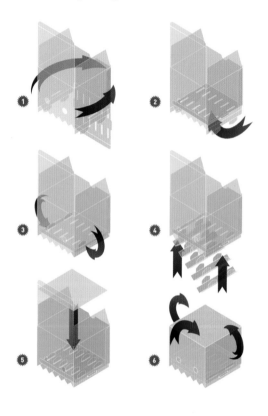

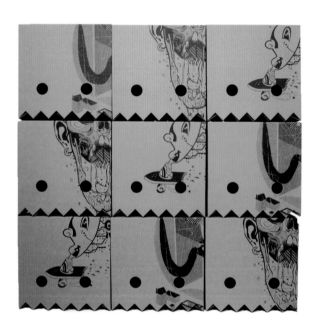

DESIGNER: Andreu Zaragoza (Spain)
CLIENT: Herokid
YEAR OF DEVELOPMENT: 2010
MAIN MATERIAL: corrugated cardboard

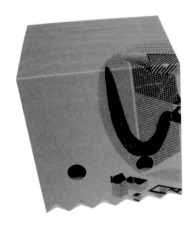

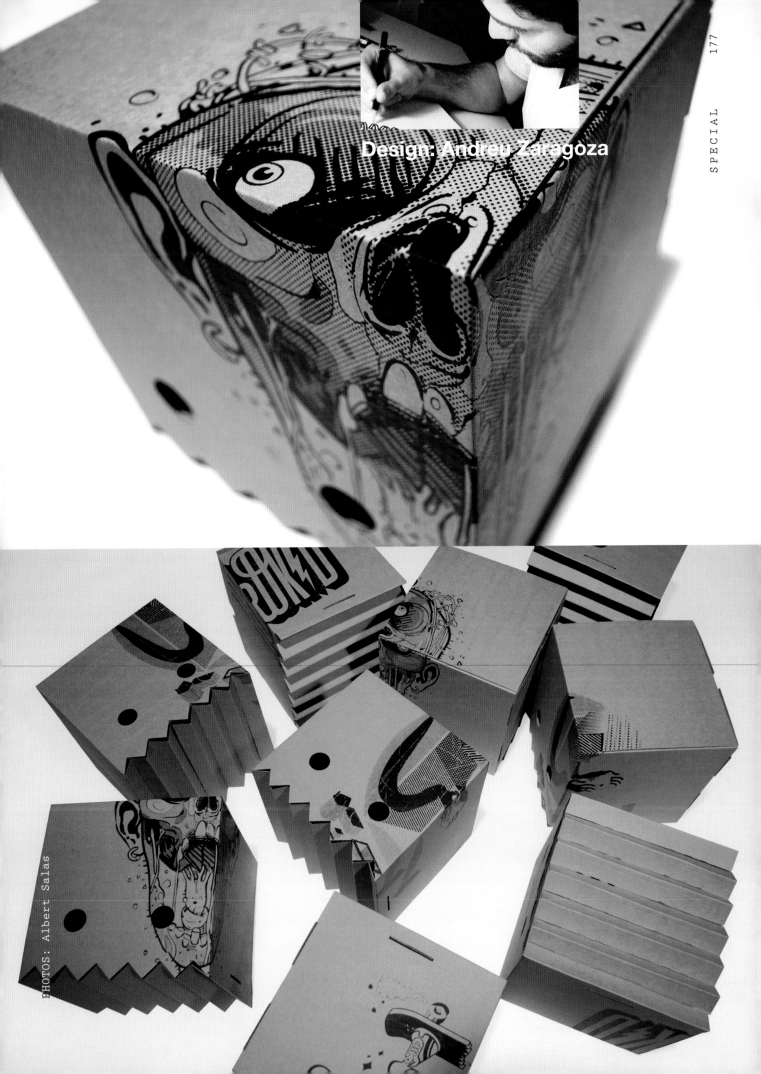

Design: Andreu Zaragoza

The Book of Genesis

The Book of Genesis is the packaging of the limited DVD edition by the Croatian rock band Hladno Pivo, with concert footage of their album Knjiga zalbe (The Book of Complaints). The DVD is placed in the central portion of the book, which comprises 350 pages of handwritten lyrics and photos of the band from the beginning of their career until now. The book resembles the real Bible, but in this case, it is a 'Bible' for the fans.

DESIGNER: Bruketa&Zinic OM (Croatia)
DISTRIBUTOR: Abus
YEAR OF DEVELOPMENT: 2009
MAIN MATERIAL: Munken Pure paper 120 g/m^3

Bryant Yee Design

Over the next decade, it is likely that the application of LED bulbs will become increasingly widespread due to their high level of energy efficiency. To reduce materials and waste during production, the assembly of this packaging design requires no glue and is constructed from 100 percent post consumer recycled paper. The designer has developed a springy, protective, interior core made only of folded paper. This interior piece cushions the new or old bulb so that it remains in place and is protected from damage during transportation. The resulting combination of a durable outer shell and a flexible inner body creates a perfectly balanced box.

DESIGNER: Bryant Yee (USA)
DISTRIBUTOR: prototype
YEAR OF DEVELOPMENT: 2011
MAIN MATERIAL: 100 percent post-consumer recycled paper

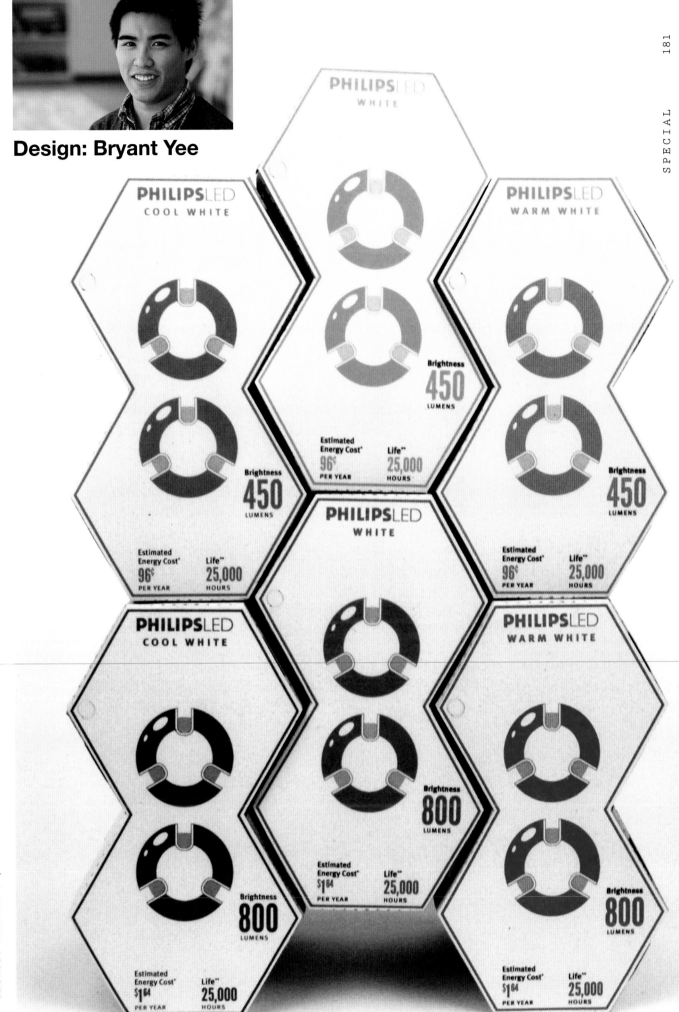

Design: Bryant Yee

Molded Paper Bottle

Ecologic Brands designs and manufactures sustainable packaging solutions. The designers commercialized America's first molded paper bottle made from recycled cardboard for Seventh Generation's 4x liquid laundry detergent in 2011. The innovative bottle consists of an outer shell made with 100 percent recycled cardboard and newspapers, integrated with a thin inner pouch, made with up to 70 percent less plastic than traditional plastic bottles. Post-use, the outer shell can be composted or recycled with paper, and the inner pouch can be recycled with plastic.

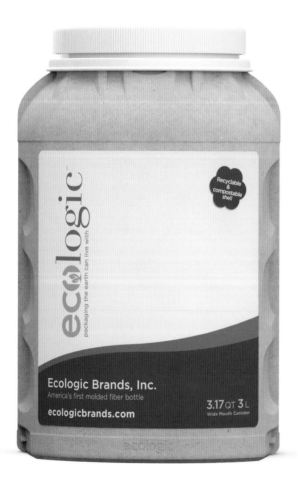

Design: Julie Corbett

DESIGNER: Julie Corbett /
Ecologic Brands (USA)
DISTRIBUTOR: Ecologic Brands
YEAR OF DEVELOPMENT: 2010
MAIN MATERIAL: corrugated
cardboard, old newspaper

Dulux Cubes

This project involved a rethink of Dulux packaging for Icon Magazine. Moving away from the traditional cylindrical container, the designers suggested a space and environment saving cubic approach. The texture and surface finishes are a reference to the paint they contain. The range of colors offer a diverse, interesting and functional end product.

DESIGNER: Anthony Cantwell / Founded (United Kingdom)
CLIENT: Icon Magazine
YEAR OF DEVELOPMENT: 2012

Biodegradable Lightbulb Box

Design: Olli Meier

The design of this eco packaging is reduced down to just the essentials: the performance in Watts, bulb fitting (E27), and bulb size. This information is worked into the package itself during assembly. The packaging is made of egg boxes, does not require any glue or ink and is 100 percent biodegradable. The shape of the lightbulb and other necessary information are included during the package-making process, making the product immediately recognizable without printed words or colored pictures.

DESIGNER: Olli Meier (Germany)
DISTRIBUTOR: prototype
YEAR OF DEVELOPMENT: 2010
MAIN MATERIAL: egg boxes

BornFree

BornFree is a world-leading brand in baby feeding products. They stand out from their competitors by using Bisphenol A-free material that is safe for babies and also good for the environment. However, their packaging and branding didn't communicate these key features. The new packaging has a clear front that allows consumers to see and choose their product. The front part is blow-molded with PETG, while the back part is molded with paper pulp, both of which are environmentally friendly, cost-efficient, and recyclable. The front and back are pressure fitted together instead of using binding material, which renders them unrecyclable.

DESIGNER: Lily Hu (USA)
YEAR OF DEVELOPMENT: 2011
MAIN MATERIAL: PETG, paper pulp

USB Flash Drive and Packaging

Stockholm Design Lab has so far designed about 100 different kinds of packaging for Askul's private brand. The company's aim has always been to distinguish the products in a clear and graphical way: clarity equals more sales. The key has been to find and use symbols that are easy for the customers to understand at first glance. In all the solutions, the designers have tried to take away unnecessary details and adding an element of fun, but above all creating a good, functional design.

DESIGNER: Stockholm Design Lab (Sweden)
DISTRIBUTOR: Askul Corporation, Japan
YEAR OF DEVELOPMENT: 2011
MAIN MATERIAL: plastic, paper

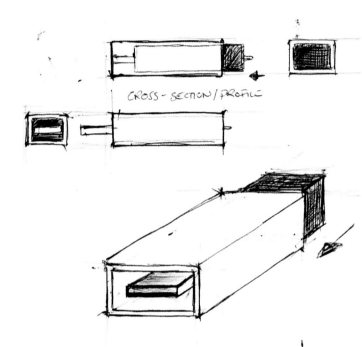

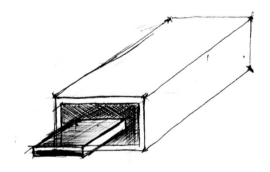

Are You Mine?

Are You Mine? is a range of jewelry cases comprising a spring/summer and a fall/winter collection. These little boxes are each made from a simple sheet of paper, which has been folded and put together without using any glue. The cases can be opened by simply pulling out the edges, revealing the gift inside.

DESIGNER: Nora Renaud (France)
DISTRIBUTOR: prototype
YEAR OF DEVELOPMENT: 2012
MAIN MATERIAL: paper

Design: Nora Renaud

PHOTOS: ATHÉNAIS MARCAIRE, PORTRAIT: YOANN MERIENNE, LYON

Ampro Design Portfolio Disc

The global economic downturn has had a negative effect on many industries, and cuts in company budgets have had a knock on effect on the packaging and design industries. This product arose from the designer's need to get more business and to be noticed quickly. Instead of producing a printed brochure, he designed this minidisc portfolio. At first glance the package looks like it contains hot sauce, cleverly referencing the idea that "great packaging is the sauce that makes the difference in the marketing mix." The designer sent the portfolio to a number of companies. The result was very positive, three new clients and an increase in interest.

Design: Irinel Ionescu

DESIGNER: Ampro design / Irinel Ionescu (Romania)
DISTRIBUTOR: Ampro design
YEAR OF DEVELOPMENT: 2009
MAIN MATERIAL: plastic, aluminum foil

Nucleus Product Launch Kit

HealthCare Insight (HCI) asked the designers to create a welcome kit for the launch of its new software platform, Nucleus. The Fraud, Waste and Abuse box, given to launch attendees, visually communicates the software's function when picked up by the handle. The box contains two brochures, a poster and a playful card deck of product features. The cards can be uniquely assembled to reinforce the company's ability to provide customizable solutions to users.

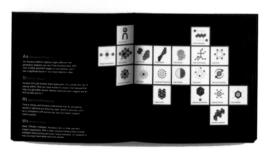

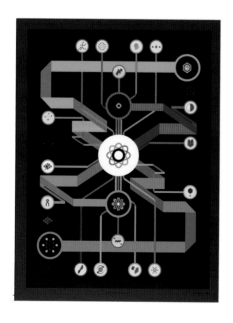

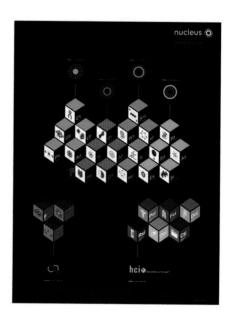

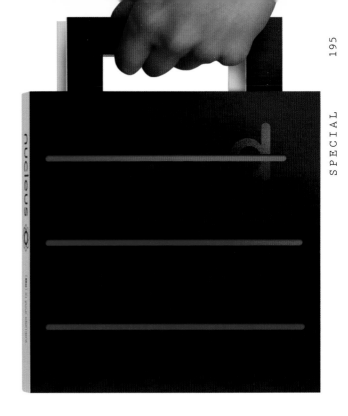

DESIGNER: Bryan Wilson, Russ Gray / modern8 (USA)
DISTRIBUTOR: HealthCare Insight (HCI)
YEAR OF DEVELOPMENT: 2011
MAIN MATERIAL: paper

ARC Mouse Packaging

A computer mouse is typically packaged under a clear blister following the contour of the product and allowing the user to check the feel and ergonomics. This package intentionally separates the merchandise from the outside world. Positioned as a lifestyle product and catered to a fashion-conscious audience the mouse is featured completely intangibly in a clear-folded plastic box to convey the premium nature and to support a higher price point of the product. Unlike any other product in this category, the mouse is placed sideways highlighting the innovative folding mechanism and beautiful product profile. The package is square, simple and iconic, split in half with the cardboard pedestal staging the product, just like a piece of art in a gallery.

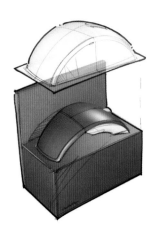
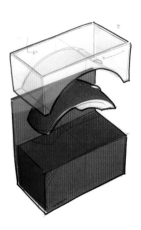
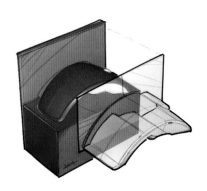

DESIGNER: Klaus Rosburg / Sonic Design
Solutions (USA)
DISTRIBUTOR: Microsoft
YEAR OF DEVELOPMENT: 2008
MAIN MATERIAL: cleafolded PET,
cardboard

Design: Klaus Rosburg

PHOTOS: COURTESY OF THE DESIGNERS. PORTRAIT: MARK BOGULAVSKY

Medicine Dispenser

This project was developed as part of the designer's degree in industrial design engineering work at the Technical University of Budapest with Richter Gedeon Ltd. as the pharmaceutical partner company. The project is a dispenser packaging design for Dipankrin medicine, which is for digestive problems. There is a 30-piece and a 100-piece version of the product. The dispensing mechanism is based on a rubber spring, which is placed outside of the plastic box. The shape and the motion of this rubber spring refers to the digestion and has become the characteristic element of the design. The pill comes out by compressing the box with two fingers; hygienic and simple to use.

DESIGNER: Eszter Kriston (Hungary)
DISTRIBUTOR: Richter Gedeon Ltd.
YEAR OF DEVELOPMENT: 2005
MAIN MATERIAL: plastic, plastic rubber

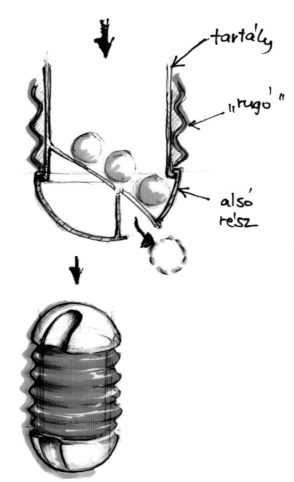

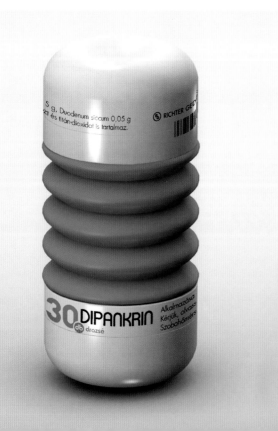

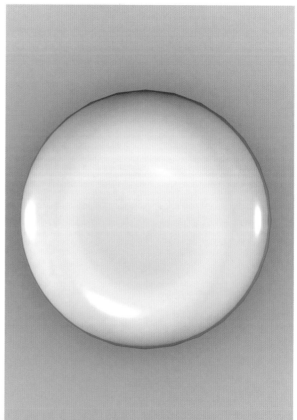

Design: Eszter Kriston

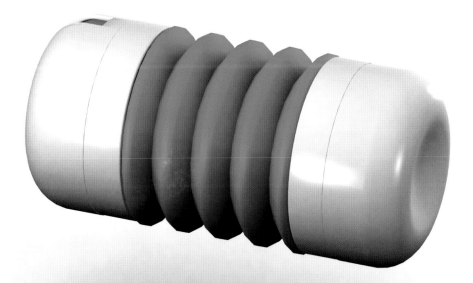

Prism Eyewear Case

Taking their inspiration from the idea of prisms and glass reflections, SabotagePKG have created a truly unique glasses case that looks like it has been carved from glass or crystal. The result is as eye-catching as the glasses themselves, perfectly complementing the Prism brand's positioning towards people for whom glasses are an important aesthetic accessory. The completely transparent two-piece, injection molded case stands upright and reflects the core idea that glasses are all about light and vision. The case design also stands apart from anything else on the market, giving the Prism brand real standout at point of sale.

DESIGNER: SabotagePKG (United Kingdom)
DISTRIBUTOR: Prism
YEAR OF DEVELOPMENT: 2010
MAIN MATERIAL: Polycarbonate & Surlyn

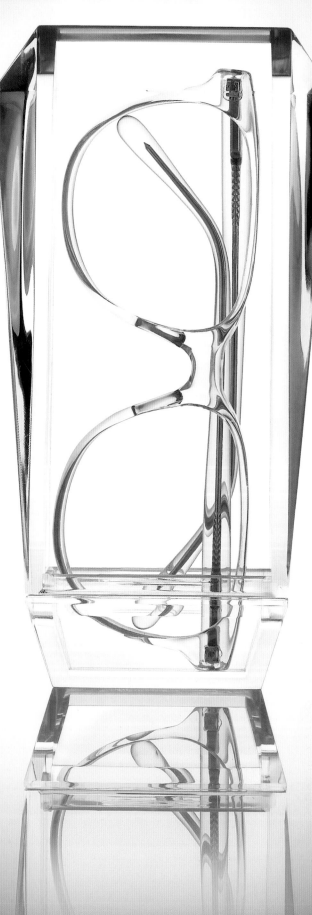

Design: SabotagePKG

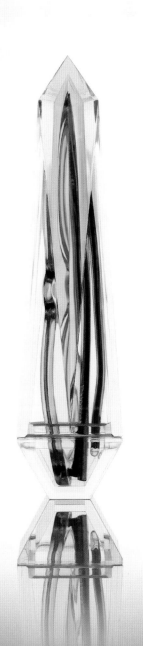

Macro-Capsule

The Mr. Propre macro-capsule is inspired by the idea of taking a pill to cure an illness; the Mr. Propre capsule can cure household ills. The two-colored design reinforces the association with a medical pill, but the colors used are brighter, making the product more eye-catching and allowing it to stand out from other cleaning products. The kit includes all the items needed for an emergency cleaning job inside or outside the home: Klucel - a water soluble plastic, detergent and a dried sponge.

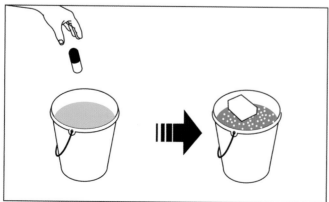

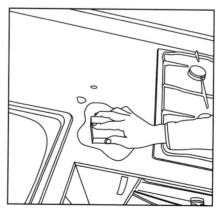

Design: Alexandre Moronnoz,
Franck Fontana

DESIGNER: Alexandre Moronnoz,
Franck Fontana (France)
DISTRIBUTOR: Mr.Propre / Procter&Gamble
YEAR OF DEVELOPMENT: 2001

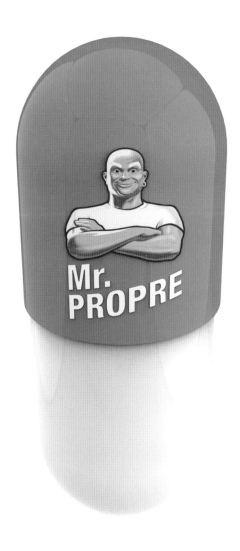

Dumb Bell

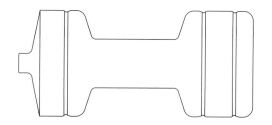

The whole communication of the Mr. Clean trademark is based on strength and concepts of physical power, well represented by the famous bald muscle man. With this dumbbell packaging, the designers have tried to find a simple but recognizable shape to strengthen that idea and to give the product more visibility on the shelves.

The designers have also considered packaging reusability as an important feature: the empty bottle can easily be filled with water or sand and transformed into a colorful dumbbell for fitness. A fun exercise booklet inside the cap can be useful for home training.

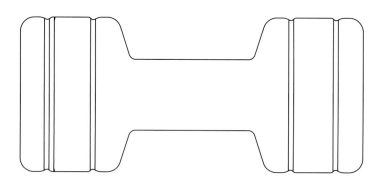

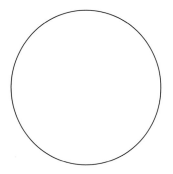

Design: Tommaso Ceschi and Francesca Delvigo

DESIGNER: Tommaso Ceschi
and Francesca Delvigo (Italy)
CLIENT: Designboom and Procter & Gamble
YEAR OF DEVELOPMENT: 2008
MAIN MATERIAL: plastic

PHOTOS: TOMMASO CESCHI, PORTRAIT: ILARIA DOZIO

Leisure

The products in this category include clothing, sporting, and amusement. They are all luxury items rather than necessities and their purchase is very much determined by the taste of the consumer. In the previous chapters, purchasing decisions were often based upon the quality of the product - a high-quality computer mouse, healthy food, juice with high fruit content, an effective skin cream - the choice of a particular t-shirt is much more personal and dependent on the consumers sense of beauty. Only the perfumes in the third chapter faced a similar, or perhaps even greater, problem in that the smell of a perfume also depends on individual taste. Furthermore, most people simply don't need the products in this chapter. It is only changing fashions and the 'must have' factor that act as purchase incentive.

Therefore the stimulation of these incentives is of the utmost importance. The packages included in this chapter are strikingly innovative and original: a swing presented in package that mimics the movement of a swing in motion, t-shirts decorated with printed pictures of food items are then packed in the corresponding food container, and a pair of rubber boots that have been given a transportation box in the form of a cardboard aquarium.

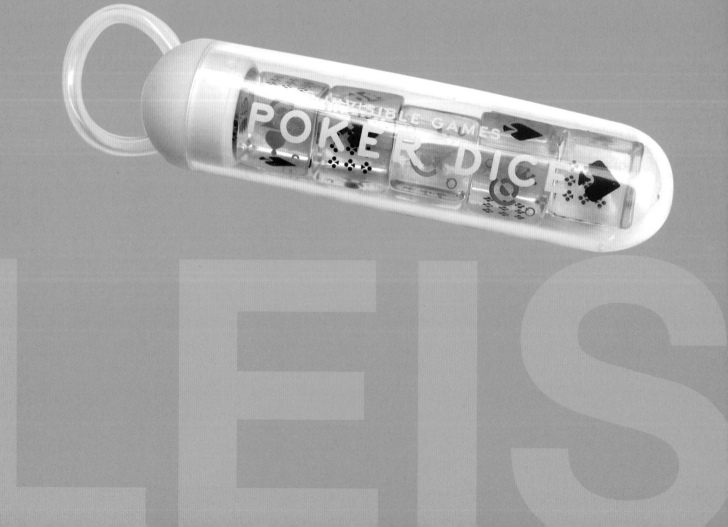

Some of the examples have been styled as storage boxes: a pair of trainers that should be returned to their plywood box after use, another pair that demand to be displayed in their acrylic case, a third example stored in bamboo tubes and marketed as an elegant eco-product, a fourth contained in a molded recyclable egg box-type container.

Packages such as these stir up desire to own the product. They act as treasure chests, and are too valuable to simply throw away, just like the sculpted perfume bottle mentioned earlier. The packaging is no longer just a part of the product that one receives for free. The package is the product.

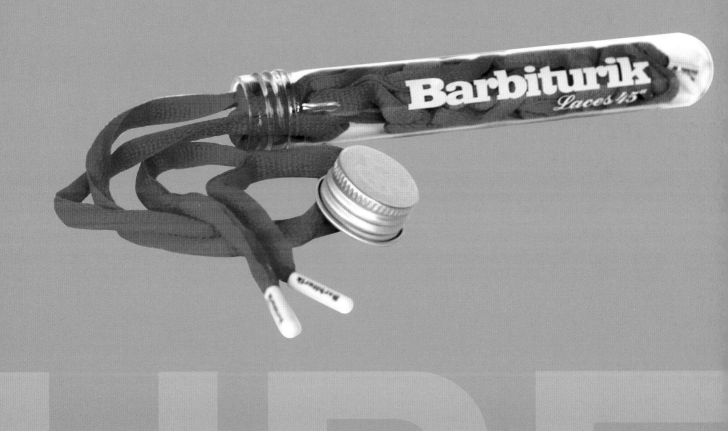

Swing Packaging "Aufschwung"

This packaging was designed by Gerlinde Gruber, for a swing called "Aufschwung" by Viennese Designer Michael Hensel. The simple and cost-effective form is made of corrugated cardboard and requires no adhesive. The open character of the design makes it optimal for presenting the product. The swing's appearance and material can be seen and touched without opening the packaging. Grip holes make it easy to carry. The packaging design is heavily inspired by the shape and function of the swing itself.

Design: Gerlinde Gruber

DESIGNER: Gerlinde Gruber Packaging Design (Austria)
CLIENT: Michael Hensel
DISTRIBUTOR: Garbage Upcycling Design
YEAR OF DEVELOPMENT: 2011
MAIN MATERIAL: corrugated cardboard

Sneaker Shoe Model No.1

The Canvas Box is a unique packaging solution created for Society27 and its first product the Sneaker Shoe. The product showcases craftsmanship and handmade quality. Plywood is a classical material, very popular in last century furniture design. The Canvas Box takes a romantic retrospective look at plywood and use it in a non traditional way. The logo cut on the top shows the product inside.

DESIGNER: Anastas Marchev, Dimitar Inchev / Archabits Studio (Bulgaria)
DISTRIBUTOR: Society27
YEAR OF DEVELOPMENT: 2011
MAIN MATERIAL: plywood

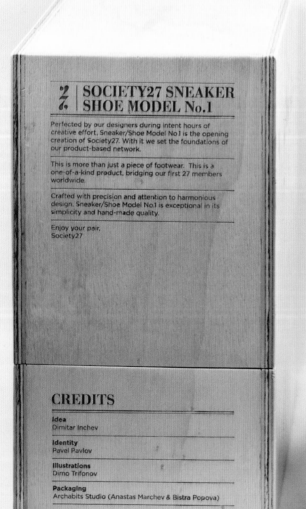

SOCIETY27 SNEAKER SHOE MODEL No.1

Perfected by our designers during intent hours of creative effort, Sneaker/Shoe Model No.1 is the opening creation of Society27. With it we set the foundations of our product-based network.

This is more than just a piece of footwear. This is a one-of-a-kind product, bridging our first 27 members worldwide.

Crafted with precision and attention to harmonious design, Sneaker/Shoe Model No.1 is exceptional in its simplicity and hand-made quality.

Enjoy your pair,
Society27

CREDITS

Idea
Dimitar Inchev

Identity
Pavel Pavlov

Illustrations
Dimo Trifonov

Packaging
Archabits Studio (Anastas Marchev & Bistra Popova)

Brooks Pure Project

CO Projects collaborated with the agency The Great Society on branding and packaging Pure Project, a new line of Brooks Running shoes. The designers came up with a complete ID system, as well as this launch kit to entice key retailers. The line is a dramatic departure for Brooks and as such, it required an equally dramatic unveiling.

Fashioned from bamboo, the kit embodies the sustainable ethos of the line. The laser-etched lid lifts off to reveal two brochures and four raindrop-shaped canisters with branded caps. The individual canisters may be removed and re-used in various ways. This kit is designed to be a keepsake with no material going to waste.

DESIGNER: CO Projects - Rebecca Cohen,
Marc Cozza (USA)
AGENCY: The Great Society
DISTRIBUTOR: Brooks Running
YEAR OF DEVELOPMENT: 2011
MAIN MATERIAL: bamboo, paper

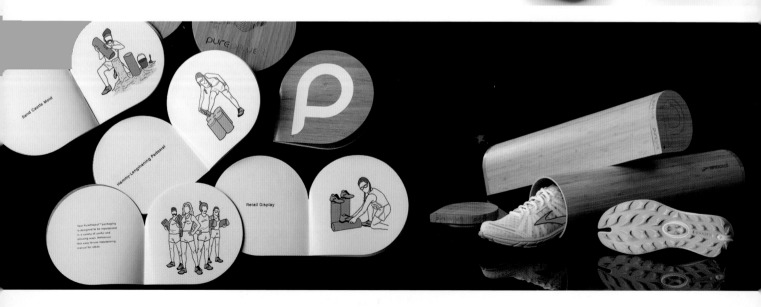

**Design: Marc Cozza,
Rebecca Cohen**

Juicy Couture Men's Fashion Retail Packaging

Juicy Couture's Men's bible box is a men's keepsake box based on the hide-a-book concept featuring silver-leafed page ends, debossed and foil-stamped logos, custom distressed textures, complete with a textured varnish to add to the layered effect as seen on weathered leather books. The overprinted inks created shadows and highlights adding to the visual depth of the finished product. The box design is brought to life via the production techniques used to create the layered effects and areas of relief creating the realistic textures of worn leather.

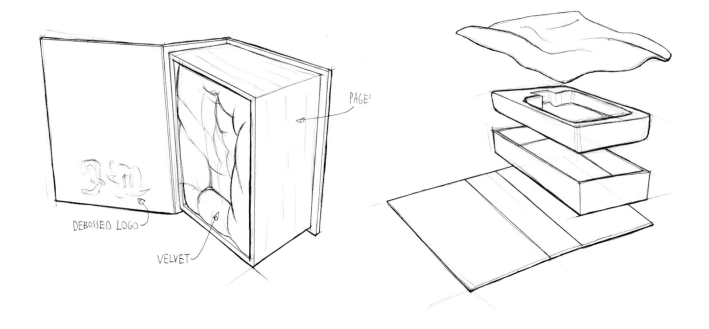

PAGES

DEBOSSED LOGO

VELVET

DESIGNER: Evelio Mattos /
Design Packaging Inc. (USA)
DISTRIBUTOR: Design Packaging Inc.
CLIENT: Juicy Couture
YEAR OF DEVELOPMENT: 2007
MAIN MATERIAL: rigid grayboard, natural
kraft paper, silver foil hotstamp, spot
varnish, black velvet

Design: Evelio Mattos

Sportline

Sportline provides a line of products for the casual athlete such as, a pedometer, heart rate monitor, stopwatch, and more. However their current branding and packaging are very generic. The new design of Sportline is fun and energetic. The designer has chosen a form that suggests both movement and stability and applied it to the packaging design. The new packaging is much easier to open compared to the original blister pack, and also has a strong shelf presence.

DESIGNER: Lily Hu (USA)
DISTRIBUTOR: prototype
YEAR OF DEVELOPMENT: 2011
MAIN MATERIAL: PETG, paper pulp

live your potential

life changing adventure.

sportline

sportline

DUO 1025
HEART RATE MONITOR

THE ADVANCED TECHNOLOGY ALLOWS FOR CONTINUOUS AND ON-DEMAND HEART RATE MONITORING.

PRICE 69.75

KEN 60
HEARTRATE STRAP

THE ADVANCED TECHNOLOGY ALLOWS FOR CONTINUOUS AND ON-DEMAND HEART RATE MONITORING.

PRICE 25.75

| calorie monitor | single button | counts steps |
| motion sensor | digital alarm | memory recall |

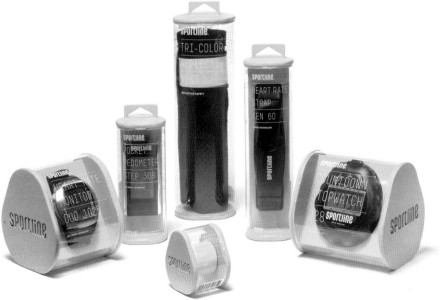

HM The Queen Elizabeth's Diamond Jubilee

This limited edition piece was produced to celebrate the Queen's Diamond Jubilee. Modeled on Buckingham Palace, the piece is over two meters in length, over 50 centimeters tall, and took over three months to complete. This is the first piece in a range entitled iconic façades, which will feature famous buildings recreated in leather to form boxes for different items, from games, to liquor, to jewels etc. The front of the 'palace' even features sentries on guard and the famous Royal balcony. When the flag pole is lifted a mahogany roulette wheel is revealed inside; this, in turn, allows access to the east and west 'wings' which reveal two full roulette layouts in fine gaming cloth with trays for 2,400 casino chips stowed away beneath. A roulette marker and Croupier's rake complete the ensemble.

Design: Max Parker

DESIGNER: Geoffrey & Max Parker / Max Parker
(United Kingdom)
DISTRIBUTOR: Geoffrey Parker Games Ltd
YEAR OF DEVELOPMENT: 2012
MAIN MATERIAL: leather, billiard cloth, sterling
silver, diamonds, crystal glass, mahogany

Café du Monde

1g2 refreshed Café du Monde's entire brand identity and created its new communications platform with a fun and friendly atmosphere, and the people at the restaurant. This café and its riverside terrace have been a favorite port of call since its opening in 1985. Anchored in the city's Old Port overlooking the Saint Lawrence, it offers a savory mélange of land and sea-based cuisine, vintage and table wines, business luncheons, and celebratory dinners. Morning, noon or night, professionals, artists, lovers, families, and friends gather here to enliven the festive atmosphere.

DESIGNER: Sonia Delisle / 1g2boutique (Canada)
CLIENT: Jacques Gauthier, Pierre Moreau
YEAR OF DEVELOPMENT: 2011

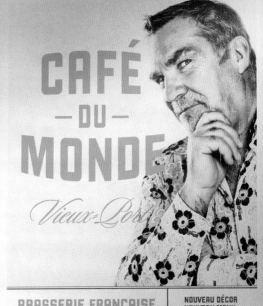

Design: Sonia Delisle

Newton Running Packaging

The Newton shoe was conceived with revolutionary orthopedic techniques and this packaging is designed to emphasize the pioneering nature of the product. The designers have created a recyclable box using the same material traditionally used for egg boxes. The box fits the shoes exactly so that no material is wasted, as is the case with the traditional rectangular shoebox.

DESIGNER: Matt Ebbing / TDA_Boulder (USA)
DISTRIBUTOR: Newton Running
YEAR OF DEVELOPMENT: 2007
MAIN MATERIAL: post-consumer waste
recyled cardboard

Together Society27 x David Sossella

Together Society27 x David Sossella is a design collaboration project. It comprises t-shirts with artwork by Italian illustrator David Sossella, packaged in a wooden cylinder made by Archabits Studio. Sossella's piece depicts 27 interconnected characters.

The packaging is made of screen-printed wooden veneer that unfolds into a piece of wall art. Top and bottom caps are used as labels containing designer's info and project identity.

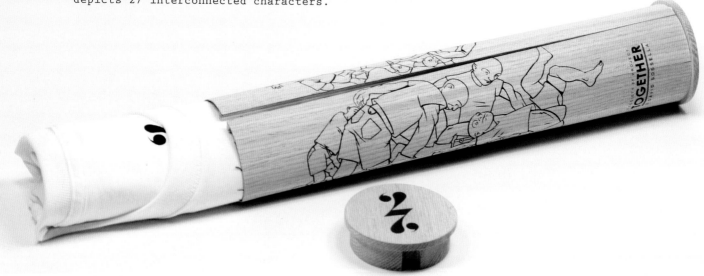

DESIGNER: Anastas Marchev, Dimitar Inchev / Archabits Studio (Bulgaria)
DISTRIBUTOR: Society27
YEAR OF DEVELOPMENT: 2012
MAIN MATERIAL: veneer, ash wood, textile

TOGETHER features
the work of:
David, Pavel, Jello,
Anastas and Dimitar

Barbiturik Lace Tubes

Barbiturik is a funky new skate brand that focuses on providing a range of energetic, fun and lively skate board products and accessories. These laces are packed as pairs into clear test tubes. This has the advantage that the product is clearly visible to all and the bright dynamic colors and patterns on the laces themselves attract consumers just as effectively as colored packaging. This design breaks away from traditional boring shoelace packaging, allowing the product to stand out from the competition.

DESIGNER: Rémy Hernandez / Barbiturik (France)
DISTRIBUTOR: Barbiturik
YEAR OF DEVELOPMENT: 2008
MAIN MATERIAL: polypropylene

Design: Rémy Hernandez

Here! Sod

Design: Somchana Kangwarnjit

Here! Sod created a new line of t-shirts that are sold in simple and distinctive packaging that resemble the packaging of food found in gourmet supermarkets. Each shirt is sold in packaging that resembles different forms of packaging. For example, 'pork' t-shirts sold in the product line are uniquely packaged to make their products more eye-catching and to create a fun and novel shopping experiences for consumers. The unique packaging created instant brand recognition amongst consumers which generated large volumes of word-of-mouth advertising.

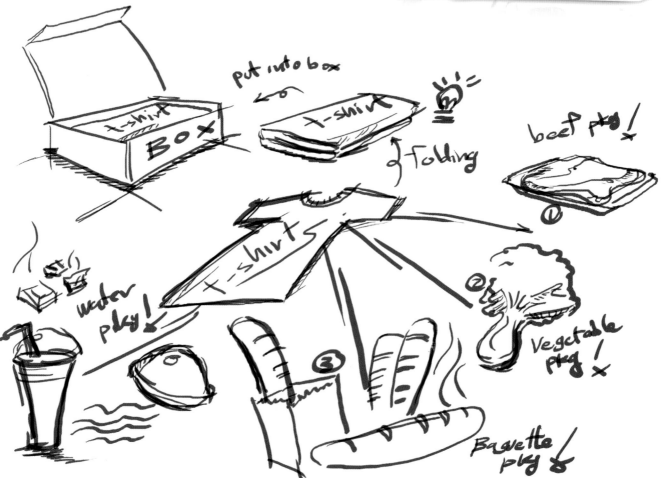

DESIGNER: Somchana Kangwarnjit / Prompt
Design (Thailand)
DISTRIBUTOR: Here! Sod
YEAR OF DEVELOPMENT: 2010
MAIN MATERIAL: fabric, plastic, paper

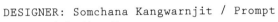

Antismoke Pack

The dangers associated with smoking are a popular topic, often discussed in both the media and society in general. Smoking bans in various countries have helped to highlight smoking-related issues and the dangers of passive smoking, but the topic is still a contentious one. This package concept aims to emphasize the health risks associated with smoking. The form of the package is similar to that of a traditional cigarette pack and fits easily into a pocket.

Design: Artyom Kulik, Alexander Andreyev

DESIGNER: Artyom Kulik, Alexander Andreyev (Ukraine)
DISTRIBUTOR: Reynolds and Reyner
YEAR OF DEVELOPMENT: 2012
MAIN MATERIAL: paper

PHOTOS: COURTESY OF THE DESIGNERS

Poker Dice

Design: Pieter Woudt

Invisible Poker Dice was designed by Pieter Woudt as an accompaniment to the Invisible Cards. The dice are made of translucent acrylic and the symbols used are similar to the ones Woudt designed for the Invisible Cards. Viktor Jondal

came up with the shape of a tube for the packaging produced by Kikkerland. The packaging is transparent showcasing the product inside from every angle. The large ring at the top of the tube allows easy use.

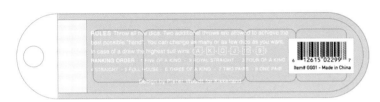

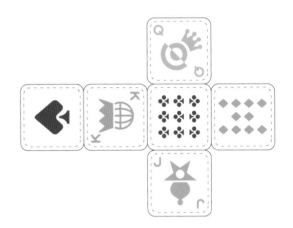

DESIGNER: Pieter Woudt (USA)
INDUSTRIAL DESIGNER: Viktor Jondal
DISTRIBUTOR: Kikkerland
YEAR OF DEVELOPMENT: 2004
MAIN MATERIAL: plastic, acrylic

PANTONE 165 C
PANTONE 306 C
PANTONE Violet C
PANTONE 383 C

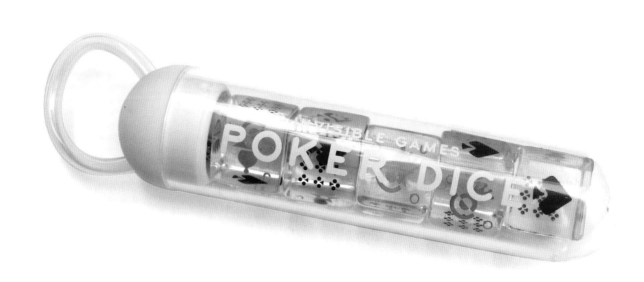

Fisherman

Everybody is aware of the primary function of a pair of rubber boots - protection from water. However, there are many advantages that are not obvious at the first glance. Fisherman boots are able to protect the wearer from a wide range of dangers: environmental debris, biological threats, natural, chemical and electrical hazards. The package itself is designed as a mini-stand and works as an eye catcher. An image of boots immersed in water draws the consumer's attention to all protective properties of the Fisherman boots.

Design: Igor Mitin

DESIGNER: Igor Mitin (Australia)
DISTRIBUTOR: Boon
YEAR OF DEVELOPMENT: 2012
MAIN MATERIAL: cardboard

PHOTOS: IGOR MITIN, PORTRAIT: IREN LOGINOVA

The Playship

Design: Pedro Machado

This is not just simple packaging - it also functions as a toy and a backpack. These multiple uses increase the visibility of the product as it can be carried around and used every day in a range of different situations. The wings allow the product to be stacked and balanced one on top of the other, making it easier to store. The product has been designed in a range of colors increasing its appeal to a wider audience.

DESIGNER: Pedro Machado (Portugal)
DISTRIBUTOR: prototype
YEAR OF DEVELOPMENT: 2011
MAIN MATERIAL: bio plastic

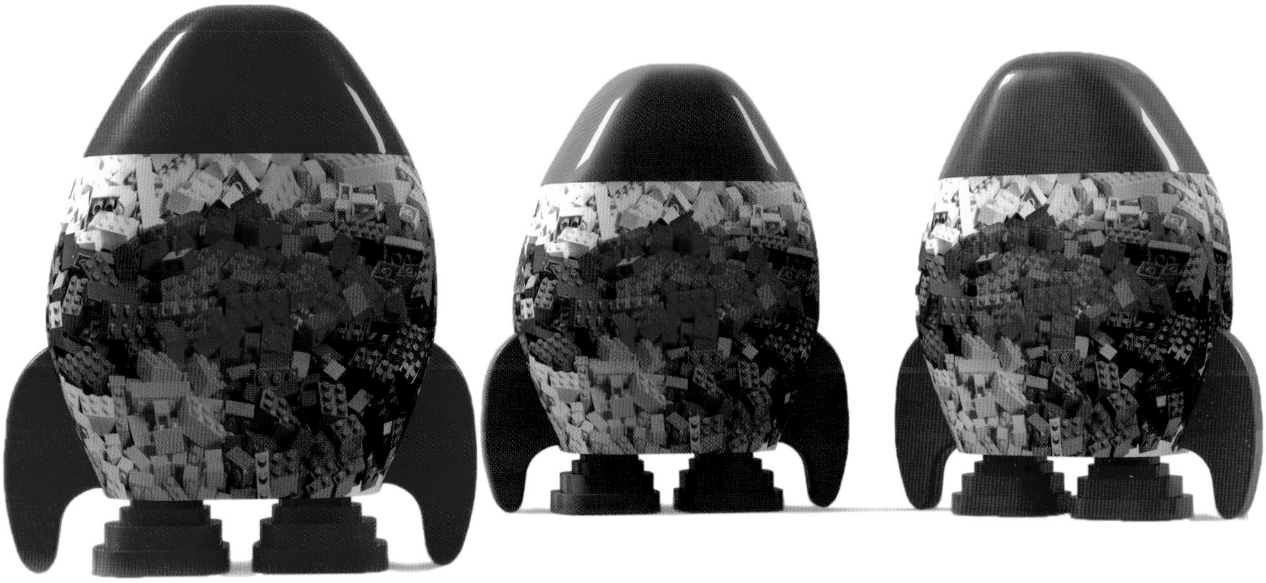

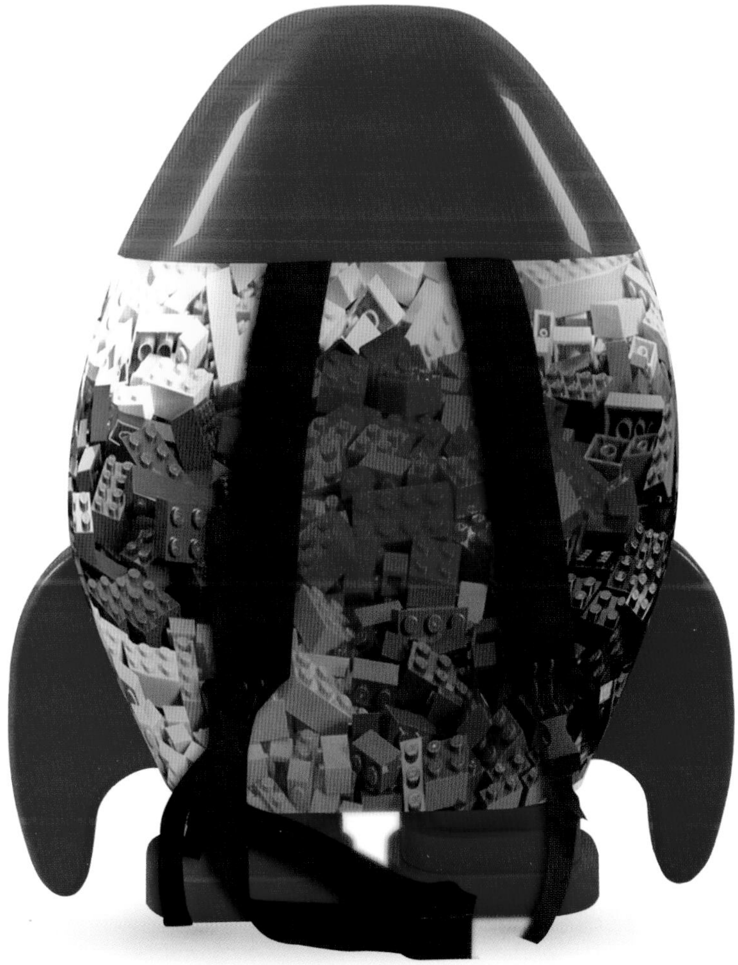

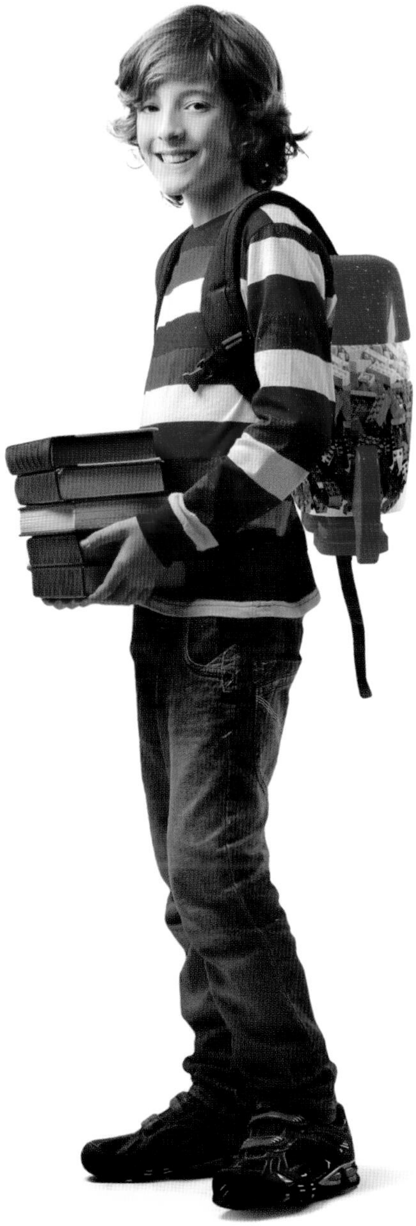

PHOTOS: COURTESY OF THE DESIGNERS

Adizero F50
Limited Edition Box

To launch the new adizero F50 boot, the
designers created 120 limited edition VIP
presentation cases, sent to celebrities,
select press and influential bloggers.
The process of opening the box is
designed to be as tactile and engaging
as possible, to enhance the enjoyment of
slowly discovering its contents. A single
personalized boot is displayed jewel-
like, held invisibly by hidden magnets.
The glow edge perspex lid slides off to
reveal a high gloss foiled inner box.
Below the customized F50 football shirt,
the miCoach components are presented
in a cut foam recess. And below that, a
secret compartment contains the matching
personalized boot.

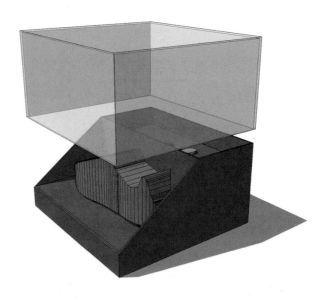

DESIGNER: Everyone Associates (United Kingdom)
DISTRIBUTOR: Adidas
YEAR OF DEVELOPMENT: 2012
MAIN MATERIAL: glow edge acrylic, laminated
board, high density foam, magnets

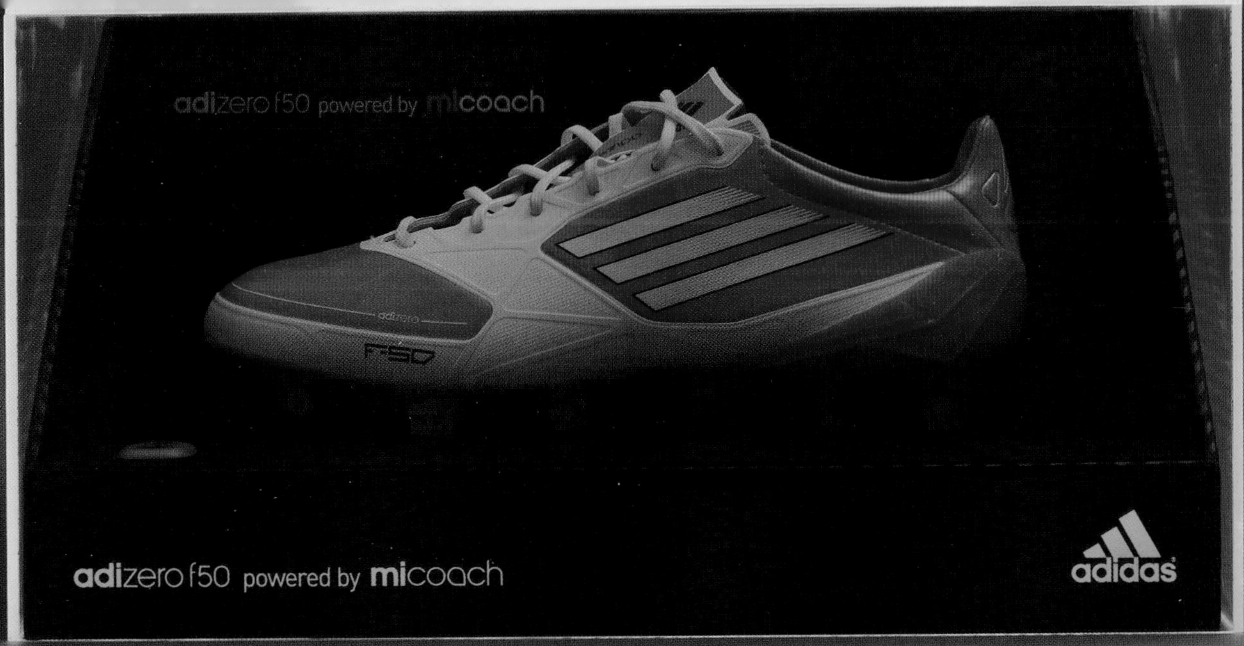

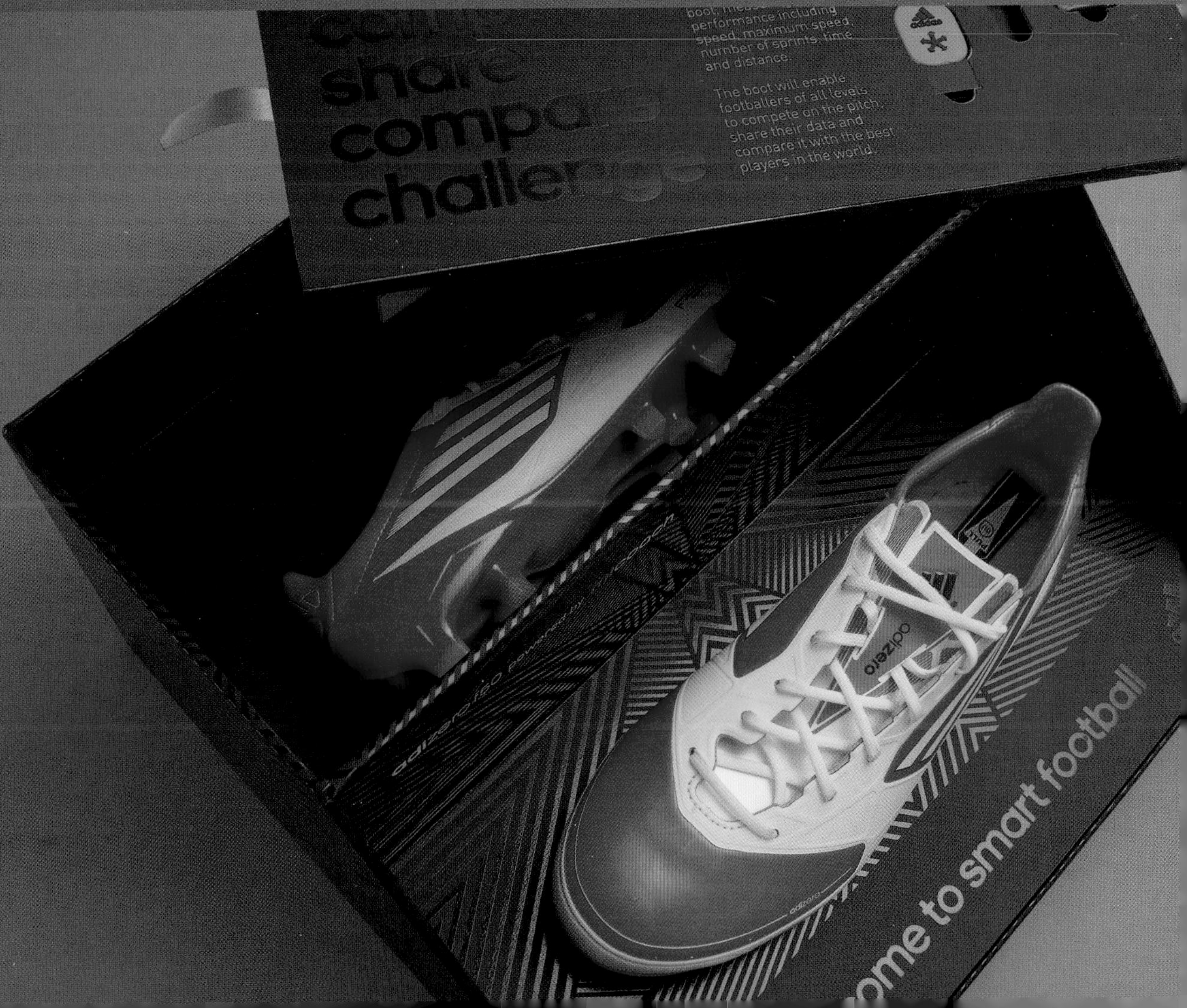

PHOTOS: COURTESY OF THE DESIGNERS

Designers' Index